THE

STORY OF THE MADIAI;

WITH

NOTICES OF EFFORTS MADE,

IN

EUROPE AND AMERICA

IN THEIR BEHALF.

COMPILED AND EDITED

BY THE

SECRETARIES OF THE

AMERICAN AND FOREIGN CHRISTIAN UNION.

NEW-YORK:

OFFICE OF THE SOCIETY,

No. 17 BEEKMAN-STREET.

1853.

D. Fanshaw, Printer, 35 Ann-street, corner of Nassau.

INTRODUCTION.

THIS Volume contains a record of the imprisonment, trial, and condemnation of two persons, in comparatively humble life, in Italy, on grounds, which seem to American minds, most extraordinary. They had come, through the reading of the Scriptures, and other means, to the knowledge of what they deemed to be the true Gospel, and had, as a consequence, abandoned the Roman Catholic Church—the established Church of Tuscany. Following their convictions of duty, they endeavored to impart the knowledge of what they believed to be the "Truth as it is in Jesus" to their friends and neighbors, beginning with the members of their household. For this purpose they read the Bible, in the Protestant version, that of Diodati's, which they very naturally preferred to that of Martini, which is Roman Catholic. In doing all this, they believed that they were not violating the laws of their country—much less those of God. They did no more than what every man in these United States believes that he has the right to do, not only from the Constitution and laws of his country, but also from the duties and responsibilities with which he is, in his very nature, invested, and from the commands of his Maker.

The intelligence of their imprisonment and final condemnation to *forced labor* in a penitentiary for long years, both astonished and grieved the hearts of millions in the Old World and the New. Great efforts were made to procure their pardon and liberation. The clemency of the Grand Duke of Tuscany was invoked, by a Deputation of distinguished Christian gentlemen from England, France, Holland, Germany, and Switzerland. The good offices of the monarchs of Great Britain and Prussia were interposed, as well as those of the President of the United States, in a kind and unofficial way, and therefore not calculated to give reasonable offence.

For a long time all was in vain, and the conclusion in many minds was that the sufferers bade fair, owing to their feeble health, to end their days in prison. But when all hope seemed to fail, the sufferers are suddenly liberated, and hurried out of the country! The pressure from without was too great for the Government of Tuscany longer to withstand.* The Madiai, at the time of this writing, are in France. The Government of Sardinia has offered them an asylum in Piedmont. They have been invited to spend the remainder of their days in Switzerland, in England, in Prussia, and in these United States. It is not known what is their determination. It would seem most natural, and therefore most probable, that they would choose Piedmont as not only their future home, but the field of their efforts in behalf of that Gospel for which they have suffered so much.

* It is said, and we suppose with truth, that the Grand Duke felt it to be impossible to resist longer the influences to which reference has been made above; but still he was unwilling to yield to the earnest remonstrances of England, as set forth in Lord John Russell's letters to Mr. Bulwer, the British Ambassador at Florence, and to appeals from other Protestant countries. In this state of things, the ex-Duke of Parma, (formerly Duke of Lucca, and himself a Protestant at heart, if not by profession,) suggested that the Tuscan Government might yield to France what could not be conceded to England and other Protestant nations. In consequence of this, Louis Napoleon was induced to ask, as a favor, the pardon of the Madiai. This favor was promptly granted; the prisoners were released, and sent as secretly and as expeditiously as possible, out of Tuscany, and into France!

This work embraces three subjects. 1. The history of the arrest of Francesco Madiai and his wife, their imprisonment in the *Bargello* at Florence, the receptacle of all sorts of criminals, where they passed many months in the society of the vilest felons. This account is extracted from letters written by English Christians residing in, or then visiting Florence, and addressed to Christian friends in England. We have good reason for saying that the simple and minute recital of facts which these letters contain is authentic, for we are well acquainted with an American gentleman of the strictest veracity, who informed himself, on the spot, of its exact truth, and who has confirmed to us that recital in every important particular. 2. The Trial of the Madiai, including the speech of the Prosecuting Attorney, Signor Bicchierai, the speech of their noble-minded young advocate, Signor Maggiorani, and the decision of the Court, as presented by Signor Nervini, the presiding judge. Thus far the work is the same as that which appeared in England, some months ago, under the title of the PRISONERS OF HOPE. 3. The last part contains a notice of what was done in Europe, as well as America, to secure the liberation of the Madiai—the noble Deputation from England, France, Holland, Germany, and Switzerland, and their proceedings; the public meetings in England and in the United States; the conduct of the Papal hierarchy and their journals, among us, etc. etc. The book closes with an account of the manner in which the Madiai were at length, through God's good providence, and in answer, we cannot doubt, to the prayers of His people, delivered from what bade fair to be a long, if not fatal, imprisonment. We have done Archbishop Hughes the justice to give his letter in reference to the matter, as well as one or two of the replies which were made to it.

This Volume we cannot but deem both valuable and opportune. It demonstrates, in an age of great unbelief, as well as material prosperity in the world, that there is still an efficacy in true Christianity which can, and will, through God's abundant grace and blessing, sustain the soul in seasons when called to endure severest persecution and bitterest trials. The examples which it exhibits to our view are most interesting and instructive in this point of view. An unbelieving age had almost come to the conclusion that the stories of the sufferings of the Martyrs partake more of the fabulous than the true. But we are here made to see that man, and even feeble woman, can still suffer for Christ, and be sustained under those sufferings.

This Volume also shows, what so many among us have been slow to believe, that Rome is the same unrelenting enemy to the true Gospel that she was in the Middle Ages. The intolerant and persecuting spirit which she has displayed in the case of the Madiai and other witnesses for the Truth in Tuscany, is precisely the same that she displayed against the Albigenses and the Waldenses of old. And as she incited the Kings of France to destroy the former, and the Dukes of Savoy, (the ancestors of the present King of Sardinia,) to destroy the latter, so now she is inciting the Grand Duke of Tuscany to destroy what she calls "Heresy," but what is in reality the true Gospel, in his dominions. It is well that the world should know that Rome *is* unchanged, and we may add, unchangeable. Wherever and whenever she has the power, she will persecute—even unto death! And what a Christianity is that! It is a base dishonor to the Author of Christianity to call such a religion by His glorious name,—in whose instructions not a word, rightly interpreted, can be found which sanctions or approves persecution.

This Volume demonstrates the falsehood of the organs and advocates of Rome, in this land, that have asserted that the Madiai were condemned for "political offences," that they were connected with Mazzini and the other republicans and revolutionists, etc. Not a word of this is true. These people had never meddled with politics; they were quiet, obedient, and loyal subjects of their prince, for whom they seem to have entertained great respect; and their only crime (to use the language of the Court which condemned them,—three judges against two,) was "impiety, committed by means of proselytism." That was all. And for that the Roman Catholic Church teaches the Grand Duke of Tuscany that he ought to doom his subjects, for long years, to imprisonment and forced labor! All this is wrong, and directly contrary to the Gospel of Christ. But what cares Rome for that? She holds that she has the right to make and enforce what laws she pleases; that she can bind the conscience; that the Pope is the Vice-gerent of Christ; that Christ has, in fact, abandoned the government of this world, at least till the Day of Judgment,—having given up all power to her as the only Church, and that she has the *right*, if not the *power*, to make new laws for the Church and for the nations, and put down and raise up whom she pleases! She has not renounced one of her ancient claims. Pio Nono would be another Hildebrand, if he could. This he has clearly intimated in his "bull" in condemnation of the writings of Professor Nuytz of Turin, issued in 1851. It is well,—it is even high time,—that our American people should know all this.

It adds to the interest which attaches to the history of the Madiai, that the events which it records occurred at FLORENCE, so dear to the hearts of the lovers of Literature and Art—to Florence, so dear to the heart of the Christian student, who loves to look back to the dark ages which preceded the glorious Reformation, and contemplate the heroic conduct of Savonarola,* who preached the Gospel to audiences

* Girolamo Savonarola was born in Ferrara, in the year 1452. From his youth he was of an enthusiastic turn of mind. He entered a Convent of the Dominicians at Bologna, and became greatly distinguished both for learning and eloquence. In 1484 he delivered a remarkable course of lectures

that filled the vast cathedral of that city, and sealed his testimony against Rome by the martyr's death. As in the days of Savonarola, so now, the ancients of Rome cannot endure that the Holy Scriptures should be known by the people. She dreads the sacred volume, and

on the book of the Revelation, at Brescia, and with much effect. Five years later he took up his residence at Florence, where he was both respected and feared by Lorenzo dé Medici, the destroyer of his country's liberties, and to whom Savonarola refused to give absolution, when on his dying bed, because he would not promise to restore the Republic of Florence, which he had overthrown.

Savonarola's powerful denunciation of luxury, and vice, and tyranny, led, for a time, to a great reformation of manners among the Florentines, and the overthrow and banishment of Pietro, the haughty and luxurious successor of Lorenzo. But the Franciscans and Augustinians, who were jealous of Savonarola, combining with the faction of the Medici, succeeded in crushing the distinguished Reformer, who had by his burning eloquence denounced not only the vices of the people, but also those of the clergy—not even sparing the Pope, the infamous Alexander VI. The Republic was a second time overthrown, and Savonarola, with two other monks, was brought to the stake on the 23rd of May, 1498. When the bishop who presided at the ceremony, with a loud voice, pronounced them separated from the "Church," Savonarola exclaimed, "From the Militant,"—intimating that he believed that they were about to enter the "Church Triumphant." Thus died this remarkable man, who has been justly styled one of the "Reformers before the Reformation."

AMERICAN EDITOR.

all who go to it alone, as the only true source of divine knowledge. She persecutes the Bible-readers of Florence,—imprisons and banishes them,—now-a-days, just as she persecuted unto death Savonarola and his followers.

It is proper to state that for the last ten or twelve years some attempts have been made to introduce the knowledge of the true Gospel into Florence, and not in vain. Even before the Revolution of 1848, many copies of the Word of God and of some excellent tracts and books, in Italian, had been circulated in and about Florence. When the Constitution of 1848 was granted, the door was for a time opened for doing a good work. Several young Waldensian ministers went down to Florence for the double purpose, of improving their knowledge of the Italian language, and to preach the Gospel to the natives who desired to *hear* it. A faithful minister of the *Free Church of Scotland* was also very useful in the good work which commenced about this time in that city.

For nine months this good work was prosecuted with vigor and success. Several thousand copies of the Bible and religious books and tracts were disseminated. But soon a sad change took place. The Grand Duke, restored by Austrian bayonets, revoked the Constitution, and religious liberty was abolished. The Waldensian ministers were forced to retire to their mountain-home. The converts at Florence were first suspected; next put under the surveillance of the police, and finally several of the men of influence among them were arrested and thrown into prison. Among them was Signor Piero Guicciardini, a nobleman of distinguished family, and universally respected for his excellent character and his great efforts in behalf of Infant Schools. Finding that he was suspected, and hoping that his withdrawal for a time from Florence might lead the government to release its pursuit of the *Evangelici*, (Evangelicals,) as the new sect was called, he prepared to set out on a visit to England. When nearly ready to leave, he prepared a statement of his religious belief, that his countrymen might know what he professed. This document is dated on the 3rd of May, 1851. On the evening of the 7th of that month, calling to bid farewell to a friend, he spent some time with a few persons, six in number, in reading the 15th chapter of the Gospel by John. In the midst of this service they were broken in upon by the police, and dragged to prison. Without trial, and simply by a *police-order*, he was banished for six months, to one of the worst prisons in Tuscany—the pestiferous Maremma. This sentence was afterwards commuted into exile from Tuscany for a year, we believe.

The admirable document of Count Guicciardini was published after he had left Italy, and created much sensation. Its sentiments and doctrines are entirely evangelical, and worthy of the Italian Protestants of the 16th century.

We bring this introductory notice of the book in hand to a close, with the following quotations from the English edition:

"Full evidence is here given that the opposition of Romanism to the Word of God continues the same, and that English Christians are only misinformed when told that "Vulgar translations of the whole Scripture are upon sale, and open to every one, in Italy itself, with the express permission of the Roman Pontiff."* Romish authorities may tell us this; but, alas! the prisons of Italy, and the sufferings of

* "End of Religious Controversy," by the R. C. Bp. Milner. Letter xlvii.

Christians there confined, bear a different and incontrovertible testimony.

"It has indeed been said that the priests of Rome have no more to do with these persecutions, than ministers of the Gospel in England have with the carrying on of *criminal* prosecutions! But what causes the possession of the Word of God to be regarded as a *criminal* charge? The dogmas of Rome, as taught by the priests (Jesuits probably) to the Tuscan authorities. If any Romanist disclaims persecution, it goes no farther than himself; he is in that particular a dissenter from his Church. So long as Rome recognises the decree of the Lateran council under Innocent III. *requiring* the temporal powers to persecute "heretics,"—so long as she authorizes "Instructions to Theological Candidates," hinting not obscurely (by *condemning the contrary as heresy*) "that it is according to the mind of the Spirit to burn heretics,"—and so long as every Romish Bishop swears that he will *persecute and oppose all heretics*,—so long shall we be justified in charging on Romanism as a system, and on its priests as the ministers of that system, the persecutions which are carried out by the secular authorities which profess that religion."

CONTENTS.

Introduction. . . . . Page 3

LETTER I.—Search of the house of Francesco Madiai, August 17.—Bibles seized.—Francesco and three others arrested.—One, an Englishman, liberated. 19

LETTER II.—Two Florentines banished without trial, simply for the confession of the Gospel.—Arrest of Rosa Madiai, Aug. 27.—Not permitted to see her husband.—Sept. 6, charge of proselyting brought against the Madiai.—False charges against Signora Madiai. . . 21

LETTER III.—The prisoners still kept in separate cells.—Difficulty of any lawyer acting for them.—Maggiorani undertakes to be their advocate —Illness of the prisoners.—An arrest through the *confessional*. 24

LETTER IV.—Increase of persecution.—Rosa Madiai very ill; not allowed to see her own doctor.—A reader of the Bible imprisoned *through his wife's confession.—Priests* employed as spies.—Severity against *Evangelici*.—Sixty said to be in prison for affairs of conscience; not allowed to see their friends!—Treated worse than murderers. 26

LETTER V.—Occurrences of the night of November 15.—D —— hears that B ——'s house was to be *visited*, and informs A ——; they go to B ——'s, and see him arrested.—They warn his brothers.—A—— finds the police in his own house; Providential deliverance.—A —— escapes from Florence. 29

LETTER VI.—Details continued.—Courage of Signora A ——; her alarm for her husband; succeeds in warning him.—Anger of the gensdarmes; repeated searches of the house.—Efforts on behalf of Rosa Madiai in her sufferings. 36

LETTER VII.—Improved health of Rosa Madiai.—Her examination before the magistrates.—Francesco Madiai sent to the Murate prison.—Interview between the husband and wife.—Refusal of bail for them.—Danger incurred by an advocate in defending prisoners. . . 38

LETTER VIII.—Reference to another case of suffering.—Two persons imprisoned through the *Priests*.—Trial of the Madiai put off till March. 43

LETTER IX.—Prayers for the sufferers.—Continued trials.—The two arrested on account of the sick man.—Florence a city quite Catholic, Apostolic and Roman.—*Evangelica* or Sabina. . . 45

LETTER X.—Preparations for the trial of the Madiai.—February 26, Sentence on the two men before mentioned. Acquitted by the tribunals, but sentenced by the police.—Extracts from the *decreto*. . 48

LETTER XI.—Carrying out of the sentence on the two men; the one banished; the other taken to Piombino to be imprisoned in the fortress. 50

LETTER XII.—Witnesses against the Madiai; ingratitude of a family whom they had aided.—April 15. The trial still postponed.—Francesco's Letter. 51

From Francesco Madiai to H. E.

LETTER XIII.—His arrival at Florence when 16.—Conduct of his Confessor.—Nineteen years of unsatisfactory ideas on religion.—Reads the English Prayer Book; goes to America; his first Communion, Trinity Church, Boston.—Returns to Florence; goes to Rome with the Misses J——; meets Rosa Pulini; she explains the Bible to him.—Marries Rosa Pulini.—His Prayers. 53

LETTER XIV. Trial again put off.—Annoyance to the Prisoners.—Francesco's calmness; Rosa's grief.—They meet for a moment. . 56

LETTER XV.—Hopes that the trial may come on soon.—Maggiorani's diligence.—Question as to the application of the law.—Rosa's improved health. 58

LETTER XVI.—The trial: commences June 5.—The prisoners meet in the dock.—The Attorney-general proposes that the trial be private.—Some have permission to stay.—Witnesses for the prosecution prepared by the priests.—Papers and tracts read.—Francesco's answers; forbidden to quote Scripture.—Witnesses for the Madiai.—Rosa's answers.—Maggiorani's speech.—Reply of the Attorney-general; he suggests the sentence to the judges.—Deliberation of the Judges, June 7 and 8.—Sentence on the Madiai.—How received by them; their separation. 59

LETTER XVII.—Rosa Madiai to her husband. . . . 66

LETTER XVIII.—Rosa Madiai's dejection of spirits; her ill health.—Maggiorani's application to the Minister of Justice.—The appeal to the Court of Cassation.—22d: Contrast between the Florentine rejoicings, at "the Feast of St. John," and the condition of the imprisoned. . 69

LETTER XIX.—Publication of Maggiorani's defence; interest expressed about it.—Bicchierai's speech against the Madiai published.—His admissions in favor of the character of the accused. . . 72

LETTER XX.—The case heard before the Court of Appeal.—The judges apparently favorable.—August 7. The former sentence confirmed.—The Leopoldine laws set aside.—A petition to the Grand Duke prepared. 73

H. M——y to N—— and L——.

LETTER XXI.—Rejection of the Petition for grace; Visit to Francesco Madiai in the Murate prison; his submission and message to his wife. —Visit to Rosa in the Bargello; her sufferings; her prayer; Her removal to Lucca.—Her message to her friends. 77

H. E—— to F. D——.

LETTER XXII.—Remembrances of visits to the Madiai. . 80

REPORT OF THE TRIAL.—Speech of the Public Minister, Signor A. Bicchierai.—Defence of the accused by the Signor Ovardo Maggiorani. 86

THE SENTENCE. 171

OPINIONS OF THE LAWYERS. 178

ADDITIONAL FACTS RELATING TO THE TRIAL. . . . 179

CONDUCT OF THE PRISONERS AFTER THE TRIAL. . . . 184

THE EFFECT OF THE TRIAL AND CONDEMNATION UPON THE CHRISTIAN PUBLIC. 189

ANSWER OF THE MINISTER. 192

ADDRESS. 194

CORRESPONDENCE BETWEEN THE DEPUTATION AND THE CONVERTS IN TUSCANY. 197

LORD RODEN'S VISIT TO THE IMPRISONED MADIAI. . . 204

PROCEEDINGS IN AMERICA.

CHAPTER I. A Notice of a Meeting in Metropolitan Hall. Statement of Facts.—Resolutions adopted.—Declarations of Principles.—Dr. Bethune's Address.—Popish Opposition.—Meeting in Newark.—Meeting in Baltimore.—Resolutions of New-York Legislature.—Resolutions of the United States Senate.—Mr. Everett's Letter. 210

CHAPTER II. Archbishop Hughes' Letter. 233

REPLY TO ARCHBISHOP HUGHES' LETTER.

CHAPTER III. Mr. Phelps' Letter. 249

Why have the Madiai been treated so cruelly? 290

Their Liberation. 299

STORY OF THE MADIAI.

BEING

LETTERS FROM FLORENCE, &c.

LETTER I.

Search of the house of Francesco Madiai, August 17.—Bibles seized.—Francesco and three others arrested.—One, an Englishman, liberated.

FLORENCE, August 20, 1851.

MY DEAR L.,—The persecutions still continue. Last Sunday, the 17th, a case of gross injustice and abuse of power occurred in Piazza Santa Maria Novella. At about half-past seven in the evening a visit was made by the gensdarmes to the house of Francesco Madiai, and, although both himself and his wife were from home, the house was searched from the ròof to the cellars; and the object of the search was revealed by the capture of two Bibles and an English book (Hawker's Morning Portion, I believe.) An Englishman had chanced to call in to see Francesco, and was awaiting his return, and there were also two other individuals waiting for him; these three were immediately arrested, and their persons searched; and the *honest* gensdarmes swore they found them reading the Scriptures.* In the meantime Francesco Madiai returned home, and he was arrested; and shortly after, all four were carried off to the Bargello, the common prison of Florence, in spite of warm remonstrances on the part of all. Poor dear Rosa, who had also returned home, behaved with her usual dignity; she encouraged her husband, saying, he had done nothing wrong, and therefore he need not be ashamed; and that she hoped he would be liberated after a few hours' detention:—thus they parted. May her hopes indeed be realized! The Englishman was kept in prison twenty-two hours, and was only eventually released through the exertion of his relations and the strong remonstances of the legation at Florence. I will not add more now, as I hope to write again very shortly, when I may be able to give you an account of the release of the other three prisoners.

Yours affectionately,

D. K.

* This was about eight o'clock; when on August 17, it is quite dusk at Florence, so that *even if reading God's word were an offence*, they *could* not have been guilty at that time.

LETTER II.

Two Florentines banished without trial, simply for the confession of the Gospel.—Arrest of Rosa Madiai, Aug. 27.—Not permitted to see her husband.—Mode of procedure against suspected persons.—Sept. 6, charge of proselyting brought against the Madiai.—False charges against Signora Madiai.

FLORENCE, Aug. 29, 1851.

MY DEAR L.,—You will be anxious to hear the fate of the three poor prisoners for the Gospel's sake, whom I named to you in my last. Madiai and the other two, who are also Florentines, were placed in seperate cells, and no one has been allowed to see them. I believe they have had several *secret* examinations; for justice in this country *now* is rarely public. The two men, after being detained in prison seven days, were offered their choice either of indefinite imprisonment or indefinite exile; of course, they chose the latter. And thus are these poor fellows, the one a shoemaker, the other a valet out of place, cast forth into the wide world as wanderers, without means, without friends, but such as our heavenly Father may raise up to them;—without trial, or any cause assigned: their crime being that they were found in the house of the Madiai, and that they both confessed the Gospel of Jesus Christ in their private examinations, and also avowed that they read the Bible.

And now comes the most affecting of all my communications, and one for which we were but little prepared: perhaps, you will scarcely believe my report, when I tell you that poor dear Rosa Madiai has been taken into custody and imprisoned! a woman—a poor sickly woman. This took place two days ago, i. e. ten days after her beloved husband's imprisonment. She also has been carried to the Bargello, where they remain in separate cells, not having seen each other since the affecting evening of the 17th. She has been unceasing in her efforts to obtain permission to see her husband, but has been invariably refused with the utmost harshness. Still we never thought it would come to this. Just see how that shameful edict of April the 25th * already works. If you have read Gladstone's Letters, you have just the manner of arrests here. Persons are taken up upon suspicion, and *then* they seek in all directions for witnesses to inculpate them. Alas, poor Rosa! How will she bear her narrow close cell? the vermin—the bugs—so numerous that they actually drop upon their persons and into their food? I will write again in a few days.

Sept. 6. To resume: for I would not send my letter without more information about poor dear Rosa. They have had several examinations, (I mean

* The edict which is mentioned in the Introduction, by which such extensive powers were given to the police, irrespective of the ordinary and legal tribunals.

separately,) but, as usual, hitherto conducted in private; and I understand that in prison they have boldly and consistently avowed themselves *Evangelici*. Under these circumstances fresh charges have been sought and made out, against the man of endeavoring to proselytise, (in this country a very serious accusation,) and against the wife, of immoral conduct. Now this infamous charge militates against the whole tenor of her life; and it only shows the rancor of the feeling against them; for really they have no offence whatever with which to charge them, except upon the ground of worshipping God in that way which they call heresy.

Yours affectionately, D. K.

LETTER III.

The prisoners still kept in separate cells.—Difficulty of any lawyer acting for them.—Maggiorani undertakes to be their advocate.—Trial not likely to come on before Christmas.—Food sent to the prisoners.—Illness of the prisoners.—An arrest through the *confessional*.

FLORENCE, Sept. 15, 1851.

MY DEAR L.—I have no favorable news to communicate. Our two dear prisoners are still confined in their separate cells, and no one, as I said before, is allowed to see them. They have engaged a lawyer to look after their affairs; but you have no idea of the difficulty, in this country, of finding any one willing to undertake the case of those accused, or suspected, of holding views contrary to the dogmas of Rome; they are so afraid of getting involved themselves; or rather, through the influence of the Government and the priests, of finding themselves utterly ruined. Several who were asked to undertake the case of the Madiai, absolutely refused, saying they had families, and they could not risk the ruin it might entail upon them. Nevertheless one called Maggiorani, has nobly and kindly undertaken their cause; he is considered to be a talented young man; at least, he has an independent spirit. We hear there is no hope of anything being decided upon before Christmas, and then great fears are entertained that some very severe punishment will be awarded them.

You will be glad to hear that a most attached and devoted friend of the poor prisoners has undertaken to send them food that they can eat, for the prison fare is so disgusting that few *can* eat it; this friend of theirs is an admirable little creature, full of heart and courage. May God reward her for her devoted kindness! Poor Rosa has been, and still is very ill; but both she and her husband are full of faith and Christian courage. Another poor fellow has been arrested in consequence of secrets obtained THROUGH THE CONFESSIONAL by means of a wife and a son! they have confessed to the dreadful crime that he reads the Bible;—he too, is in solitary confinement. * * * * * * *

Yours affectionately, D. K.

LETTER IV.

Increase of persecution.—Rosa Madiai very ill; not allowed to see her own doctor.—A reader of the Bible imprisoned *through his wife's confession.*—*Priests* employed as spies.—Severity against *Evangelici.*—Sixty said to be in prison for affairs of conscience; not allowed to see their friends!—Treated worse than murderers.—Their confession of the Gospel in their examinations.—*Source* of the trial to the Madiai; a servant in the *confessional.*—Continued desire for the Bible.

FLORENCE, Sept. 22, 1851.

MY DEAR L.—I should have answered your kind letter immediately, but I have been so very unwell, not to say ill, that I felt it quite impossible to use either head or pen, and one needs to be so well in these trying times and circumstances. I hope that you received my letter in which I gave an account of the fresh persecutions; they are so increased in severity, that it is impossible not to have sad forebodings for those now in bonds. Francesco has now been in prison more than five weeks, Rosa almost four; and nothing is as yet decided. The same severity continues; and no one is allowed to see them. Poor Rosa is very ill; she very much wishes to be allowed to see her own doctor, but is not permitted to do so. Poor I—— is also still in prison, and nothing is known of him. There is another man in prison THROUGH THE CONFESSION OF HIS WIFE; she, poor thing, did not intend to betray her husband, but it was dragged out of her that he read the Bible; and though the gensdarmes found nothing, not even his Bible, they nevertheless carried him off to prison. This is another instance that the PRIESTS are spies of the Government.

The severity against the *Evangelici* is increasing every day; spies are watching all the suspected houses. Were two even found together reading God's precious Word—for that crime they would instantly be marched off to jail. We heard to-day that sixty are in prison for affairs of conscience; were they murderers they might be permitted to see their friends, but in matters of conscience, greater severity must be used, and they are denied this consolation. How gladly, alas! would I give your sympathizing message to the dear prisoners in bonds for truth's sake, had I any means whatever of doing so; for truly it would cheer their hearts to know how many have fellowship with them in their sorrow. In general, all that passes within those gloomy walls partakes of the stillness of the grave. Still, we do hear that, in their examinations, they boldly confess their faith, and that really they implicate themselves. Like all the rest, they decidedly declare that they do not belong to the Roman Catholic Church. When asked—Did they try to convert? They replied—No one can convert but God. Still, if any one asked us what we thought of such and such a passage, we simply told our belief. Francesco is in a most spiritual state of mind; he truly glorifies his Master.

When the Government has finished with these, they will, most probably, lay their hands upon others. We have at length found out the *source* of all this trial to the Madiai—a servant, who had lived with them some time, and whom her mistress thought to be converted. T—— thought the same, but S—— and I did not; in fact, there were very different judgments about her. When this girl was discharged from the service of the Madiai she went home to the neighborhood of Lucca, and her mother-in-law found out that she had prohibited books, and IN THE CONFESSIONAL made this known. The girl was called up, and either through fear or bribery, (the latter we rather think,) she has betrayed all that she could betray: thus you see, the PRIESTS have an interest in condemning, and the Government to please them will do their worst. No one knows how many witnesses they have contrived to get, nor of what kind; but all this long time they have been occupied in trying to get depositions to make out a case. Are you not tired of these details of sorrow? Nevertheless, they work the peaceful fruits of righteousness. The desire for the Bible is more earnest than ever; the desire to understand it more ardent than ever.

Yours affectionately, D. K.

LETTER V.

Occurrences of the night of November 15.—D—— hears that B——'s house was to be *visited*, and informs A——; they go to B——'s, and see him arrested.—They warn his brothers.—A—— finds the police in his own house; Providential deliverance.—A—— escapes from Florence; danger of arrest at the gate, and deliverance.—Reaches Leghorn.—His escape by sea.—His wife's trials on that night: the search; her Bible.—Books seized.—Many arrests on that night.—The condition of the Madiai.

FLORENCE, Nov. 27, 1851.

MY DEAR L.— * * * I now begin my detail of the occurrences of Saturday night, Nov. 15th, and especially respecting one very dear to many, whose courage, generosity and devotedness, cannot be surpassed. May the Lord grant that it may reach you in safety.

A—— is a schoolmaster, and gives lessons in Italian, Latin, &c. in every case of difficulty he was always ready to put himself forward for others. He, as well as his interesting wife, are Christians. On Saturday night at about eleven, a friend of his called D——, was in a café, and heard that B—— was to have a perquisition in his house, and that many others also were to be visited; he rushed with incredible speed to A——'s house, who was in bed and told him what he had heard. A——immediately threw on some clothes, and without stopping to hide away his own things rushed out of his house, saying, "Perhaps we shall be in time to save or help B——." In ten minutes after he had left, six carabinieri were in his own house, and they would have arrested him in bed. He and D——went to B——'s house, and in his eagerness, he rang violently at the bell; as he received no answer, he rang again—no answer: they thought, perhaps, he was concealing some papers; but D——said, "Do not ring again, perhaps they are already there; let us hide ourselves in a corner." They had not concealed themselves many minutes when the door was opened, and they saw their friend looking very pale, in the midst of four carabinieri led off to jail! To finish this case, not one single thing was found in his house, not even the Bible; nevertheless he is still in prison, as they call it, upon suspicion, and there he may remain, who knows how long?*

A—— and D—— immediately went to the café, to warn his two brothers, but they found no one there; they then returned, and soon after met the two brothers of B——, who were going to their brother's house; they were told what had occurred,

* The result of this case was, that B——, on other alleged grounds, was sent to Elba, to be imprisoned in a fortress for one year.

and advised to go and see if anything was doing at their own houses. *One* found, from the lights in various apartments, that his house was also invaded by the gensdarmes; of course he did not go in; or he, also, would have been marched off to prison.

After this, A—— thought he had better return home, and said, in a kind of careless way, "It would be singular if they were in my house, too." Again, a third time, God's protecting hand was over him. D——'s dog ran forward, and, in order not to lose him, he ran after him, and in stooping down to catch him, was in such a position as to observe, to his great surprise, lights in A——'s sitting room, at two in the morning; he, therefore, stopped A——, whose hand was on the bell, saying, "Do not ring, they are also in your house; rather make your accustomed whistle, and your wife will hear you. He did so, but received no answer; and then he whistled a second time, and soon after they saw a hand slowly waving them away; also, in a few minutes, his maid-servant opened the door, and said, Fly, fly." When the door was opened without a ring at the bell, A—— thought it was one of the gensdarmes to take him, so he rushed away. D—— heard the message, and ran after him; in the hurry the little dog was left behind, and began to bark on the stairs. But I will continue A——'s story. At the corner of the street the two friends parted, and D—— was obliged to go to his own house to arrange his affairs. A——

having no money in his pocket went to a friend and borrowed a little: as he again passed near his own house, he met a gensdarme, sent to arrest him, who stopped close to him. He immediately lifted up his heart in most earnest supplication to the Lord, to deliver him, and had the presence of mind to turn his back to the gensdarme, and calmly light his cigar; the man, after a few minute's hesitation, walked on.

Poor A—— then made for the nearest gate, and again he prayed earnestly, before calling to have the gate opened, thinking they might arrest him there. But the Lord again delivered him. The man said, "*Felice notte;*" to which the other most cordially replied, "*Felice notte.*" A—— says, that once out of the city, he breathed more freely. You may imagine the conflict of thoughts and feelings which passed through his heart on that sad night! his wife, his three little children! his country, that he loves so deeply, thrusting him from her bosom, solely because he reads and spreads God's Word and religious books.

He kept on walking between the two gates, outside the walls, for some time, almost frozen with cold: at last, overcome with fatigue, he lost all consciousness, but was aroused by hearing the clock strike *three.* He then thought he would walk on to the first station; but as we have lately had a flood, the water and mud prevented him, and so he was obliged to retrace his steps, and at *five* he threw himself into the train for Leghorn, where he arrived at *nine* on Sunday morning. About the same time, my faithful N. N. told me the events of the night, as far as he knew them.

I felt sure that A—— would go to Leghorn, * * so that N. N. was sent off by the first train to know what he thought of doing. We could get no tidings till Monday morning; you may imagine our anxiety all the day. On Monday we learnt that he was safe, and that he wanted some clothes immediately, for he hoped to get off soon. A few hours after we heard from another, that it was quite impossible to get him a passport; the messenger was sent again, and his friends had the joy to hear that he was *on the sea;* the *how*, it is impossible to tell—it would be too dangerous; suffice it to say, that it was one of those remarkable interpositions which, when they do occur, look more like romance than truth. There was not time even for him to get his clothes. But our gracious Father, who has so marvellously delivered him, will still care for him. May all these sorrows and trials be blessed to his soul.

His dear wife has had much anxiety. On that fatal night, ten minutes after her husband had left, she heard a loud knocking at the door; being uneasy, she herself looked out of the window, and asked, "Chi è?" The wretches replied, "Amici." But

WHAT friends? "La polizia." She refused to open, saying, her husband was out, and she was alone; but they insisted, and she was obliged to obey. Six of them came at once into her room, and searched in all directions. She only thought of her nice large Bible, and, in order to save it, threw it out of the window, as she thought, into the garden; but, unfortunately, it fell into a cistern of water. She afterwards rescued it, and tried to dry the leaves, but a second visitation from the police obliged her to throw it into the fire, and burn it. The only things they found were, seventy of a second edition of Count G——'s Confession, six of Gladstone's Letters, and Lucille,* in Italian; but for this, if arrested, he would probably be sent to the galleys, and hard labor!!

The gensdarmes have been four different times to the house, always in the dead of the night—the last time at two in the morning. They hunted the

* A work by M. Adolphe Monod, of Paris. There is an English translation, entitled, "Lucilla, or the Reading of the Bible." Whoever is acquainted with this book, must know how obnoxious it is to those who wish to hinder God's Word from being read, or who deny that the Spirit of God can, and does, teach the individual Christian how to understand those things which the Scripture contains. One of the most important points, with regard to "Lucille," is, that the facts and arguments are strictly true; the only fiction employed is, the introduction of such names and localities as shall conceal the real parties.

roof, garden, and every possible place for her husband. All this has, of course, made her very unwell, especially as she had hardly recovered from her last confinement. That night numbers were taken from their bed to prison! Some say sixty; some, more; but as nothing is made public, who can tell? The next day we continually saw men carried to prison. One of the gensdarmes had a Bible in his hand, and numbers with little parcels of new books. The injustice of the Government, and the misery of the people, is almost beyond endurance. La Signora Madiai, about a week since, was supposed to be dying in prison, but she is still alive, and getting better, though in bed, in prison. Her husband glorifies God by his sweet Christian spirit.

Yours affectionately, D. K.

LETTER VI.

Details continued.—Courage of Signora A——; her alarm for her husband; succeeds in warning him.—Anger of the gensdarmes; repeated searches of the house.—Efforts on behalf of Rosa Madiai in her sufferings; she and her husband seen by a few.—Persecution seems to deter none from reading the Scripture.—Determination of Landucci to put down the "heresy."

Florence, Nov. 28, 1851.

My dear L.—I now give a few more details which I was obliged to leave out yesterday; I well know what a deep interest you all take in these sad persecutions, and how earnestly you bear these dear sufferers upon your hearts. How remarkably in this history do we see the protecting hand of God over his servants, probably in answer to the many prayers so constantly offered. The dear wife of A—— showed such courage in her trial; when the six gensdarmes were making their search, her great anxiety was about her husband, thinking he would surely return and be taken; however she listened most attentively to all they said; they took down notes of all they thought would criminate A——, but, excepting the books I have named, nothing was found.

They asked with great eagerness when her husband would come home; she replied she could not tell, that sometimes on Saturday he passed the night at the villa of some of the friends of his boys, which is true; these gensdarmes were in the house with this poor creature alone from eleven to three. Whilst she was sitting with them, she says she lifted up her heart often to God to protect her husband; at two, when she heard his well-known whis tle, she was ready to faint, expecting that the next moment the bell would ring, and that she should have the agony of seeing him, whom she so much loved, carried off to the Bargello; still she dared not move, it seemed as if some invisible force held her down; at length she heard a second whistle, and as the men were busy writing and talking together, she arose and said, "Excuse me, I think my baby wants me;" and went into another room, where not daring to open the window, she made the sign which was so providentially seen by D——; she also said to the maid, "Creep down stairs quietly and say, fly, fly." This succeeded, but the dog unfortunately was left in the passage, and began to bark. The chief officer immediately called out, "Whose dog is that?" Madame A—— said, "Oh! the door must have been left open, and some dog is come in;" then turning to the maid, said, "Go, and shut it, but mind, be attentive if your master should return;" the poor thing did not know what to say, the officer at once understood the whole affair; turning quite black, *nero—nero*—and stamping with his feet, he said, "Ah! yes, I dare say he will take pretty good care not to return." The gensdarmes soon after went away.

The whole of that night this poor creature had to pass in the most cruel anxiety. They have since searched the house three different times, and threatened her, and tried to frighten her; she has now, I am happy to say, gone to her father and mother; as to the school, it must, I suppose, be given up; but the Lord will care for them.

Poor dear Rosa Madiai continues so weak and ill that, perhaps owing to the strenuous efforts made on all sides in her favor, (for she was well known, and loved by some of the first families here and in England, they may let her out *to die.* Her illness is entirely occasioned by the severities of her imprisonment, upon a very delicate constitution. She may *die*, but she will never deny her Saviour, or make one retrograde step; no one but God can know how very deeply she has felt her trial, and how greatly she has suffered; it is so cruel not to let the poor husband and wife meet under these trying circumstances.

Francesco Madiai loves his wife so very tenderly, that *that* is *his* only trial; he says, even if they burn his body, it is only his body, they cannot touch his soul. Quite lately the prison doors for these two have been opened to a very few, I long to see them, but am not likely to do so.

The question naturally arises, in the midst of these persecutions, are any deterred from reading the Word and following Christ? We have not heard of one even; the only difference is, they cannot meet together; but the work being of God, who can put it down? It is said that Landucci, the Minister of the Interior, has declared that he will put down the heresy, even though his fate should be that of the Duke of Athens.*

Yours affectionately, D. K.

* This historical reference would be familiarly understood at Florence. In 1341, while the Florentines were negociating with Mastino della Scala, Lord of Verona, for the pur-

LETTER VII.

Improved health of Rosa Madiai.—Her examination before the magistrates.—Francesco Madiai sent to the Murate prison.—Interview between the husband and wife.—Refusal of bail for them.—Danger incurred by an advocate in defending prisoners.—Case at Pisa.—Prisoners for *opinions*.—Case of *four* such.—A——'s letter to his wife.—His voyage.

FLORENCE, Dec. 24, 1851.

MY DEAR L.— * * * I am sure it will be most gratifying to you to hear that our Heavenly Father has heard the many prayers offered, so far as in His wisdom He hath seen right. Both

chase of Lucca (which he then held,) the Pisans seized that city by force. The Florentines to gain possession of Lucca had sent to Robert, King of Naples, for aid, and troops accordingly came, under the command of Walter de Brienne Duke of Athens. He arrived in 1342, just when the Florentines were openly disaffected to those whom they had set at the head of the affairs of the republic. The military command was at once given to the Duke, who then executed many who were obnoxious either to the great men, or to the common people; others were exiled, and others heavily fined. In the then state of discontent at Florence, this rendered the Duke popular with all except the middle class of citizens. Having occupied Florence with foreign troops, he caused (Sept. 8, 1342) a proposition to be made to the people that the administrative power should be given to him for *one year*; the people with acclamation decreed it *for life*. The Duke and his companions abused their power in every way; no one's life or property was safe. At length those within prison, and those without are, I may say, mercifully sustained, and a shield of protection seems to be thrown around them which surprises all. Rosa Madiai, who at one time was thought to be dying in prison, has been wonderfully restored to health; at the time of her sickness and acute suffering she had an extreme longing to be removed from prison, but now her patience is restored, and she is quite willing to wait God's time, and is cheerful and happy and full of firmness and faith. She has lately prayed earnestly that her weak body may be strengthened, lest her accusers might impute her bodily weakness to a less firm and determined resolution, at all costs, to abide by her confession of faith.

A few days since she was again called before her judges, who asked her if she was the person accused of impiety and blasphemy. "If," she replied, "to believe on the Lord Jesus Christ as my only Saviour be this, then I am the person, but let God judge." All the prisoners have lately been declared criminals,

he caused the tongue of Bettone Cini to be torn out, for speaking of him too freely, and this act of cruelty (which occasioned Bettone's death) roused all Florence against the Duke. (July 26th, 1343.) The Duke, besieged in the palace, abdicated, basely surrendering his companions to be put to death, on condition that he should be conducted safely to Casentino. (Sept. 6.)

Thus "the fate of the Duke of Athens" expresses the ignominy of one who is expelled for lawless cruelty, and purchases his life by selling his associates to be executed!

and are to have, I am most happy to say, a *public* trial. In consequence of this the men have been transferred to another prison,* but Rosa, perhaps because she is so very weak, is left in the Bargello.

Great interest was made that the husband and wife should meet before he was removed, and they did meet in the presence of the jailer; they had not seen each other since the 17th of August. It was sadly affecting, for the husband also has been lately ill, and is very much bent from suffering; he has, I am sorry to say, a liver complaint, which close confinement greatly increases; they encouraged each other, and were thankful to be counted worthy to testify for their Lord and Master whom they love. The *highest* interest has been exerted on their behalf to let them out on bail, but they are criminals and cannot be let out of prison. Now they desire to get the best defence they can, and we think Maggiorani, though young, will prove as able an advocate as any. In this country it is difficult, for a man may ruin himself in defending another. It was only a few weeks since that a lawyer in defending a case at Pisa, observed upon the ill conduct of a gensdarme,

* Francesco Madiai was now sent to the Murate prison, which is professedly on the plan of that at Pentonville; the Pentonville prison, however, is for those who have been convicted and sentenced; whereas Francesco Madiai was subjected to this severe and solitary confinement preparatory to trial.

and though perfectly true, he has been sent to prison for twelve months. How then can we expect men to risk so much? Nevertheless every effort will be made to get the best pleader. The day of the trial is not yet fixed, for they like to keep them in prison as long as possible. It is quite sure that whatever the skill of the defence may be, the sentence is already fixed! But the trial will arouse public opinion.

The report is that the prisons are full, and mostly with persons put in for *opinions;* many are what are here called Liberals, but what in our country would almost be called Conservatives; most of these poor fellows read the Bible, and *some* of them, through the grace of God, have become true Christians.

I heard a few days since a touching story of four of them. They had been kept in prison for eight months unjudged, and were then tried and found guilty and sentenced to a year's hard labor; they were reproached for being *Evangelici*, and for having been present at a religious meeting; they replied that if they had been, they would have confessed it, for they were children of the Gospel. How many more such may still be suffering in bonds, unknown to us.

I will conclude this letter with the sequel of A——'s story. I related how wonderfully the Lord had shielded him from danger, and had put it into the heart of a Christian Captain to take him with him. A—— has written one of the most beautiful letters I ever perused, to his wife. When on board, he says, he prayed; oh! how he prayed—he felt as if he had never prayed before, and he earnestly entreated his wife to cast every burden on the Lord; his trials, together with the manifest goodness of the Lord, have awakened in his soul feelings which he had never felt before, and have deepened those that he had. All indignation, so natural to his character, seems quite gone and changed into the deepest sorrow for his beloved country, and the most earnest prayer for her deliverance.

They encountered storms at sea, and at one time were nearly lost, still he had not one moment's fear —he was ever calm and peaceful. The ship did not intend to go to Q——, but owing to contrary winds they came within sight of the land; the captain then asked him if he would like to be landed? he replied, "Yes." Accordingly he was landed one night alone, on that far distant shore, poor fellow! yet his heart was full of gratitude for his deliverance, and of thankfulness for the great kindness he had received; he had a letter to some kind friend there, whom he happily found, and now he is provided for; in course of time probably his wife and children will follow him.

This touching letter has been read by some of A——'s friends, not many, and yet the police have heard of it, and the wife was obliged to get rid of it to a stranger who is not suspected, to keep for her, for she could not burn it.

And now, beloved L——, farewell. Tell our

friends that they have comforted and sustained many hearts by their prayers and sympathy. It is a sweet and precious thought that you have so kindly remembered, before the Lord, all who so greatly need to be remembered, and that so many dear to Christ are fellow-workers with Him in this service; there is great need for a continuance of your prayers, that the light may not be quenched through the wiles of Satan and evil men.

Yours, affectionately, D. K.

LETTER VIII.

Reference to another case of suffering.—Two persons imprisoned through the *Priests*.—Trial of the Madiai put off till March.—Arrangements for A——'s wife and children to join him in February.—January 21. The two persons acquitted by one court.

FLORENCE, January 20, 1852.

MY DEAR L.—I hope you received my last, detailing a new case of suffering—two persons arrested at the sick bed of a friend, it is true they imprudently let the PRIESTS know their sentiments, and in a very short time after both were in the Bargello; as yet we have not been able to get tidings, but we hope to hear something this evening. I am sorry to say the trial of the Madiai is not likely to come on now before March.

If the trial is printed, I will be sure and send you

a paper; we mean to go and hear it if it is public. Maggiorani, who is thought to be a first-rate pleader, has undertaken it, though *every one* is quite certain that the sentence is already determined upon, and as events have taken such an adverse turn we fear greatly; but they cannot go beyond the will of the Lord. These dear persons have already made much progress in spiritual life since their imprisonment, so that I hear that it is a real refreshment to see them; I never hope to have this comfort, because fresh orders have been given not to admit visitors.

I hear that A—— is extremely liked at Q——, but they say that when alone his spirits sink very much, he is so attached to his wife and children, as well as having a most *ardent* love for his country and a great desire for her moral improvement. I am happy to tell you that arrangements are in hand to send his wife and two little boys the beginning of February; the little one at nurse will be left in the care of its relations.

* * * * *

I am so thankful to think that the circumstances which caused such sorrow and trial here have been a link to unite Christians together amongst you; I quite believe we have an abundant answer to your prayers; there is more grace to endure, more quiet steady determination to follow on to know God.

* * * * *

January 21. Yesterday evening we heard that

one court had absolved the two men I spoke of; it is well, however, to remember that two courts also absolved Guicciardini and the six arrested with him, but they were, nevertheless, afterwards punished by the police, so we fear it will be in this case.

Yours, affectionately, D. K.

LETTER IX.

Prayers for the sufferers.—Continued trials.—The two arrested on account of the sick man.—Florence a city quite Catholic, Apostolic and Roman.—Arrangements for A——'s wife and children to join her husband.—Case of a woman whose husband is in prison; reviled for believing in God.—*Evangelica* or Sabina.

FLORENCE, January 30, 1852.

MY DEAR L.—I cannot express to you how much it rejoices my heart to hear that you so continually remember all the dear persecuted ones at Florence, and that such a Catholic spirit is exhibited; that so many dear to the Lord join in sympathy, prayer and help. Be assured, dear L. they feel the effects of your prayers according to God's own will, not in deliverance *out* of oppression, but in His granting grace to endure, and in their increased courage to confess Christ as their only Saviour.

Feeling, as I do, the oneness of spirit which unites us, I always desire to let you know when any fresh sorrow and trial happens, that you may be able to present those things before our Heavenly Father, and thus help them in their time of need. The poor little flock continues to be so driven about, persecuted, exiled, imprisoned, that one's heart would almost fail did we not know that God is stronger than man, and that man *cannot* go beyond God's will. The two men arrested on account of the sick man are still in prison, and will probably be exiled, but when? One of them is known to have fetched the Swiss minister to the dying man, and this is a *very great* crime, and moreover he has declared himself Evangelical, and that Evangelical he will remain. The magistrates say they will *not* have such people in Florence—a city quite Catholic, Apostolic and Roman; they are determined to put down the heresy.

You will be glad to hear that A——'s wife and her two children will now soon join her husband; she has had no difficulty in getting her passport, which they were almost afraid would have been refused her. Poor thing! she goes away with many mixed feelings; delighted to go to her beloved husband, and yet it seems as if taking a last farewell of mother, father, country and friends; still to be free to bring up their children according to their own faith is a great blessing.

I am afraid the Madiai's trial will not come on before March; but they seem to increase in patience and faith, and submission to God's will. This is a blessed fruit of tribulation. *Addio* for the present.

Saturday. I heard last evening that a woman whose husband is in prison, had again been examined by the Delagato, this functionary, like many others, regularly abuses the poor people, and he was not at all sparing in bad names to her; she has a good deal of intelligence, and answered very well. She asked to have her husband's watch to put it in pawn. "Oh, you pretend to be poor do you?" She happened to say that God would help her; "Oh, you, then, are one who believes in God?" Fancy a magistrate saying this in what is called a Christian country. "I dare say you are *Evangelici?*" "No, Eccellenza," she replied, "I am called Sabina." She quite understood what she was saying.

Thus you see, dear L. the state of Florence at present. There is much, very much to be thankful for, and much to keep one in constant prayer and dependence upon God, for each day we know not what may happen next.

* * * * *

What can we say to a Government, which instead of seeking to improve the people, tries in every way to corrupt them, and by every bait to tempt them to become spies; there are many affecting instances of these temptations when driven almost to despair by want or oppression, and then they fall into the snare.

* * * * *

Yours, affectionately, D. K.

LETTER X.

Preparations for the trial of the Madiai.—February 26. Sentence on the two men before mentioned. Acquitted by the tribunals, but sentenced by the police.—Extracts from the *decreto*.

FLORENCE, February 2, 1852.

MY DEAR L.— * * * There are now long folios ready for the Madiai's trial. Maggiorani is said to be an able pleader; if he does justice to his subject, it will indeed be a most interesting trial, but can he know his Bible sufficiently? Now they say it cannot come on until the end of March.

* * * * *

February 26th * * We are greatly in hopes that the trial will now come on soon, for all the lawyers have finished some little time, and it only remains for the Government to fix the day.

* * * * *

The two men who were imprisoned on the sick man's account eight weeks ago, have received their sentence. The Tribunale della Prima Istanza entirely acquited both; then the police, under that edict of April, 1851, condemned both—one to be *forever* banished Tuscany, the other to six months' imprisonment in the fortress of Piombino. I send you a few sentences extracted from this last *decreto*. "The existence of a secret association is proved, to insinuate and spread sentiments and principles contrary to the fundamental dogmas and precepts of the Roman Catholic Apostolic religion, with the scope of overthrowing more easily, by this means, the actual political order of the different States of Italy. * * * It is evident the part that the young man has taken in this plot to alter the religion of the State; his own confession affords an undoubted proof of his apostacy; declaring that he belongs to the Protestant Evangelical sect, many Anti-Catholic books found in his possession, and his repeated attempts, as imprudent as they are detestable, to hinder the dying man from having the succors of our religion, and for having instead, procured him the assistance of a pastor of the Evangelical Reformed Church.

* * * * *

The old man is charged * * * * with the impiety of his frequent visits with the young man to the house of the sick man, during the illness of this same sick man; and the old man's confessed apostacy, professing himself a follower of the Evangelical Reformed worship * * * his co-operation in machinations to overthrow the religion of the State * * * * on this account they are sentenced," as before mentioned.

* * * * *

Your remembrance of the poor persecuted ones is quite touching; the Lord judges the heart and sees the desire to sympathize and help; indeed, the friends in England have been a great blessing to the

5

tried ones here, for surely blessing in answer to prayer is no small boon.

Yours affectionately, D. K.

LETTER XI.

Carrying out of the sentence on the two men; the one banished; the other taken to Piombino to be imprisoned in the fortress.

FLORENCE, February 28, 1852.

MY DEAR L.—* * * I told you in my last the condemnation of the two persons on account of the sick man. The old man has been allowed a week to settle his affairs; he has behaved very well —most firm and courageous. The Government refused the petition for the punishment of the other to be commuted into exile, so to-morrow morning he is to be conveyed to the fortress of Piombino. The poor mother said, with big tears rolling down her cheeks, "to think that my son should be conveyed all across the town, and to Piombino, in the midst of carabinieri, like a common felon;" we tried to comfort her by recalling how the Apostles, and even our Lord himself had been treated, and that no shame could attach to this, that it was rather an honor to suffer so distinctly for the Lord's sake We understand that he has answered with the utmost boldness and decision, refusing to answer what he did not choose to answer. These things make one feel the reality of one's faith, how in the midst of all, God gives his peace, and his sustaining grace; how brightly shines out the faith of these poor people. The numbers increase every day, I hear; and it is a great refreshment, I am told, to watch the progress of many of these dear Christians.

Yours affectionately, D. K.

LETTER XII.

Witnesses against the Madiai; ingratitude of a family whom they had aided.—April 15. The trial still postponed.—Francesco's Letter.—Day named for the trial, April 27.

FLORENCE, March 20, 1852.

MY DEAR L.—I told you that the large folios had been written for the trial of the Madiai; when for the first time it was ascertained who were the witnesses against them. Besides that wicked girl from Lucca, a family have come forward against them whom they rescued from the most abject poverty; though certainly not rich themselves, they supplied them continually from their own table, and were unwearied in recommending them, on account of their poverty, to the compassion of others; but these ungrateful creatures have brought forward some of the strongest evidences against them; false witnesses of course they are, and this either through fear, or for gain. I should think the latter, for the family are suddenly become very well off; there are many others, taken from the lowest class, but always from among those to whom they had shown kindness and compassion! Alas! alas! . . .

April 15th. You see March is ended, and still the trial is not come on; and these poor creatures are still lingering out their lives, in their solitary cells, but still sustained by our Heavenly Father. I accidentally saw a letter of Francesco's the other day, which a friend had translated; it so shows the guilelessness, and simplicity of his character, that I will enclose it for your perusal.* Never for one moment has this poor man been cast down in his spirit, his body has often suffered, but it is one continued outpouring of praise and thanksgiving to God, to think that such as he should be counted worthy to suffer for Christ; his long imprisonment tells upon him, poor fellow, for his face quite twitches with nervousness, and yet such calmness, such joy, such submission; truly it must be a privilege to see him. I should think that all who came near him, must feel the silent power of his testimony. It is now positively said that the trial will come on on the 27th of this month. May it be so; and may this long and sad imprisonment shortly afterwards be ended.

Yours affectionately, D. K.

* See the following Letter.

LETTER XIII.

From Francesco Madiai to H. E.

His arrival at Florence when 16.—Conduct of his Confessor.—Nineteen years of unsatisfactory ideas on religion. —Reads the English Prayer Book; goes to America; his first Communion, Trinity Church, Boston.—Returns to Florence; goes to Rome with the Misses J——; meets Rosa Pulini; she explains the Bible to him.—Marries Rosa Pulini.—His Prayers.

Now I wish to tell you something in a few words, but as I am very ignorant, I pray you to pardon me. At the age of sixteen I came to Florence to be cured of a liver complaint; I was cured by Professor Mazzini, who afterwards ordered me to eat meat every day. Easter falling soon after, I went to perform my devotions in the Cathedral; and having eaten meat, as the doctor had ordered me, I wished to tell this to my confessor. Accordingly, I went to a canon (whom I have already named in my examination.) When he heard that I had eaten meat, he turned on me like a barbarian, saying, "Thou art damned in body and soul," and then shut to the door in my face, so enraged was he. From that time, I was nineteen years without knowing of what religion I was: still, however, I went to Church, but I did not feel that I was satisfactorily performing my Christian duties. The time now came when I went on my travels, and the Holy

Scriptures were made a little known to me; and although I understood them very imperfectly, I saw that the Priests had deceived me. At last I was able to read a little of the English Prayer Book, and then my mind became calmer. I now went to America to see my brother, and I had there forty lessons in the English language. Then I was almost entirely persuaded of the truth of that religion, and I made my first communion in Trinity Church, Boston.* This was in 1840: but all this was still but little for me, seeing that I understood so imperfectly the English language.

I now returned to Florence, and there met the Misses J—— with a governess. I accompanied them as courier, to Rome. We left the governess and took La Pulini (afterwards my wife.) We then went on to Naples, and afterwards returned to the Baths of Lucca, where we spent the summer. I took with me a small box of English books, which I showed to La Pulina, and she exclaimed, "What good books thou hast got there!" I asked her if she would explain to me a few chapters of the Holy Scriptures, and she said she could do so after tea, as during the day-time she had much work to do for the ladies. After tea then I used to read a chapter, which she explained to me in Italian. You may imagine with what pleasure I heard explained the word of God for the first time. Then was there

* One of the Episcopalian Churches of that city.

nourished in me more and more the love of the Scriptures, but still I professed nothing.

We went afterwards to Florence, and there we parted with La Pulini. She dwelt not greatly in my imagination, but in the evenings I thought of her and her good explanations.

Not long afterwards I left my situation, and married Rosa Pulini; and I may in truth say that the Spirit of God reigned in me and my wife; but we did not yet know His secret; but I am certain we knew it after some time, and sure I am that we became very zealous for the Word of God, and so shall we ever be (God willing.) Amen.

I should like the Misses —— to be told that I send them my grateful thanks for their kindness and bounty to me: I have no other recompense to offer them. I wish them to know that from the time I first knew them, I ever felt towards them much attachment, (such as a servant ought to have for his employers.) I forget no one; I pray for my enemies; and especially do I pray for all my brethren, and for those who have shown us so much kindness. I pray God to shower down upon them His most precious blessings, temporal and eternal.

FRANCESCO MADIAI.

March, 1852, Murate Prison.

LETTER XIV.

Trial again put off. — Annoyance to the Prisoners. — Francesco's calmness; Rosa's grief.—They meet for a moment.

FLORENCE, April 28, 1852.

MY DEAR L.—Alas! alas! I have nothing but disappointment and sorrow to communicate, but I will begin my story regularly. At nine o'clock yesterday morning the prisoners were severally brought from their different prisons, and lodged in different rooms to wait until called for. Many persons interested in the case were in court at an early hour. After waiting some time it was said, that the cause must be put off for a few hours, but that it would come on at *three*. Numbers left and returned at that hour, but after waiting some time they were at last told that the case was put off indefinitely, in consequence of the illness of one of the principal witnesses. Few believed in this illness, but thought it was only an excuse for some sinister purpose, so little is there of integrity and justice in the country now.

You may imagine the vexation and disappointment this occasioned to all; but how much more to the poor prisoners themselves! Maggiorani had to communicate these sad tidings to them. In doing so, he tried to cheer them with a hope, which perhaps he hardly felt himself, that it would be merely a month's delay. Still, to go back to prison, in the same uncertainty in which they had been kept there long long months, was no small trial.

Francesco received the news with his accus tomed calmness and resignation, merely saying, "The will of the Lord be done." He had, during that long day, occupied himself in walking up and down the horrid room he was put into, repeating Psalms, chiefly the CXVI. Rosa received the intelligence with great grief—she was completely overcome by it, for she had so buoyed up her hopes, she had so looked on to this day, as ending her uncertainty, and perhaps secretly hoping it might put a term to her dreadful imprisonment. I must not forget to tell you, that once during the day the poor husband and wife met for an instant. They were confined, as you know, in separate rooms, and guarded; but both doors happened to be opened at the same time, and they rushed into each other's arms. They were again instantly separated; but the comfort of this moment's interview greatly consoled them. All night long poor Rosa has been ill—she has now fever, and is suffering greatly. They need your prayers.

Yours, affectionately, D. K.

LETTER XV.

Hopes that the trial may come on soon.—Maggiorani's diligence.—Question as to the application of the law. —Rosa's improved health.

FLORENCE, May 20, 1852.

MY DEAR L.— . . . It is still hoped that the trial will come on during this month, but if not, it will surely be early in June. In the mean time the advocate, Maggiorani, is using the time most diligently, in seeking out other important witnesses for the accused. It is evident, from all we hear, that the Government is determined to make the worst case possible against the prisoners. The most impartial lawyers affirm that the law of '86, upon which they pretend to judge them, is *not* applicable to the case; nevertheless, we fear all will be overruled to please the priests. Francesco still continues in a most lovely and tranquil spirit. Rosa is greatly better in health, and is again become peaceful in her spirit. I will add no more, for in a few days I hope to give you the results of the trial.

Yours, affectionately, D. K.

LETTER XVI.

The Trial: commences June 5.—The prisoners meet in the dock.—The attorney-general proposes that the trial be private.—Some have permission to stay.—Witnesses for the prosecution prepared by the priests.—Papers and tracts read.—Francesco's answers; forbidden to quote Scripture.—Conduct of both the Madiai.—Proceedings against them last two days.—Witnesses for the Madiai. —Questions put to Francesco as to his religious profession.—Rosa's answers.—Maggiorani's speech.—Reply of the attorney-general; he suggests the sentence to the judges.—Deliberation of the judges, June 7 and 8.—Sentence on the Madiai.—How received by them; their separation.

Florence, June 8, 1852.

My dear L.—I hasten to send you a few lines to make you acquainted with the result of the trial of Francesco and Rosa Madiai, after nearly ten months' close imprisonment. It commenced on the 5th, and ended this day at half-past three, P. M. For some time before, Rosa had manifested great calmness and rest of spirit, and seemed much more than usually happy in the Lord.

On the morning of the 5th of June the long expected trial of Madiai and his wife commenced; they were placed in the dock, guarded by several gensdarmes on each side of them; they looked calm and dignified, and quietly awaited the entrance of the lawyers, and bench of six judges, who acted as jury, as well as judges. Francesco appeared much pleased at once more seeing his wife, and pressed her hand. The attorney-general opened the case, and first proposed that the trial should be private; this being agreed to by the judges, the court was cleared of all the reporters, and most of the Italians; several English, and some of the Italian Christians, were allowed to remain, about eighty or one hundred having, like myself, obtained permission from one of the secretaries to stay; and there were also a great many priests present. Witnesses for the prosecution were next examined by the judges, and in a way that clearly showed the sentence on the Madiai had already been determined on. Words were often put into witnesses' mouths when they seemed at a loss, and they professed to remember nothing when their evidence was contrary to the written statement which had been taken down from their lips on previous examinations. I could not but be astonished at the bare-faced shamelessness with which the bench thus carried on the prosecution. All seemed to have one body and one mind, owing to the way in which they had been prepared by the priests.

In the course of this examination Count Guicciardini's confession of faith was read out, and many tracts which had been found in the Madiai's rooms were also read out in full; and a picture likewise found there which represented the errors of Popery contrasted with texts of Scripture, was produced, and the texts, &c. which were in English, translated into Italian. Thus, much truth reached the ears of the judges and audience. Francesco also frequently quoted Scripture when he was asked about his religious opinions, and this made the judges very angry, and the president frequently forbade him to quote the Bible, as they did not wish to hear his religious dogmas. Nothing could exceed the Christian behavior of both Francesco and Rosa. *She* was very particularly sustained, and all who heard her frequently exclaimed in a whisper, with how much dignity and propriety she gave her answers, especially when one of the judges wished to confuse her by a series of irrelevant cross questions; several times she silenced him by her replies, amidst evident sensation throughout the court; and once he threw himself back in his chair in complete confusion, when she was declaring in what her change of religion consisted. Madiai also, in questioning some of the witnesses, spoke to them in a very Christian and even tender way, lamenting their unfaithfulness and the falsehood they uttered. To one he said, "Go, my chains are of much greater value than all the false evidence which thou hast given against me." Upon which the president of the court, in a rage, told him "not to make a martyr of himself, and not to utter one word more than was necessary, especially before a Catholic public."

The examination against them lasted two days,

and some clever legal men declared that there was not *one word* or incident which in any way rendered them guilty—supposing even all that had been said against them was true. Afterwards the judges examined the witnesses for the Madiai, and their manner of giving testimony was a striking contrast to that of the witnesses against them, as they spoke boldly, and fearlessly, and openly, and proved by the manner of their giving evidence that they were speaking the truth; they proved that the Madiai had ever respected the opinions of others, and had by no means attempted to proselyte to their own opinions, *in the manner that their accusers contended*—for conversion, they said, can only be from God; moreover, this testimony brought to light most beautiful traits of Christian love and conduct in the accused, and nothing appeared which could in any way dim the integrity of their private life. In the course of the defence Madiai was asked "if he was not born in the bosom of our Holy Mother, the Roman Catholic Church?" He answered, "Yes, but I am now an Evangelical Christian." "Who made you such, and does any act of abjuration exist in the hands of those with whom you have united yourself?" "My convictions have existed for many years already, and they have acquired strength through the study of the Word of God; it is a thing entirely between myself and God, which nevertheless was openly manifested when I took the communion in the Swiss Church." Rosa replied to her interrogator that "she had not lightly changed her religion, or to please man, since in that case she would have done it in England, where she had lived for sixteen years; but that, after having read much, and studied the Word of God, and compared it with the doctrines of the Roman Church, she had remained convinced, and had abandoned that Church; and that she had chosen the moment to make her public confession of faith, by taking the communion, when the laws gave and protected the liberty of citizens." (This must have been in 1848.)

There were twelve witnesses against, and six for, the Madiai; and finally Maggiorani, the counsel for the prisoners, closed the case, by making a speech which lasted three hours; setting forth first the legal question, then quoting from the Fathers, and largely from the Scriptures, in proof of the soundness of the doctrines they held, and that they should not be treated as heretics; and then closed with an analysis of the evidence against them, and completely showing how false it all really was. The attorney-general replied, and ended by advising the judges to sentence the prisoners, Francesco to fifty-six months' imprisonment and hard labor, and Rosa to the same for a period of forty-six months, and both to solitary confinement. The court was then closed, and all went away, and notice was given that sentence would be pronounced on the following day.

The bench deliberated that same evening for three hours, without being able to come to any conclusion. The next day at ten o'clock the whole place was filled with persons of all classes; the bench had already been deliberating since nine o'clock, but half-past two came, and still they could not agree, and we began to hope for a favorable sentence; at length, at half-past three, after nine and a half hours' deliberation, the judges entered the court. The president read a long paper, recapitulating the evidence, and then quoted a law which in no-wise applied to the case; and finally pronounced sentence on the Madiai for transgressing it! I was sitting, at this time, in front, with several friends, and turned to look at the prisoners, who were only two or three paces distant from me. They were perfectly composed, and manifested a most remarkable degree of resignation.

It now appears that the cause of the long deliberation of the judges was, that they could not agree; some desiring a milder sentence, and the president himself, at length, gave the casting vote for the condemnation of the accused. The sentence was (to the astonishment of all) exactly that which had been asked for by the attorney-general, viz: Francesco Madiai to suffer four years' and eight months' solitary confinement and hard labor, and Rosa three years and ten months of the same. The ten months which they had already passed in prison, were not to be reckoned as part of the sentence. Besides this, they are to be subjected to three years' surveillance of the police after the term of their imprisonment is ended. (The surveillance of the police is most harassing; they enter your house as often as they please, during the day or in the dead of night. You must show yourself to them, whether you are sick or well, and must never be out of your house after eight o'clock in the evening, &c.) All the expenses of the trial are also to be paid by the Madiai. The prison selected for him is at Volterra. She is sentenced to the Ergastola, at Lucca—a most dreaded prison.

At the close of the sentence both immediately arose from off their seats, and looked at each other, as if greeting one another after many months' absence; they then shook hands, both smiled on each other, embraced, and in a few moments disappeared amidst the bayonets of their guards. I may mention, in conclusion, that the sole accusation against them was one grounded upon their open confession of the name of Jesus, and desire to lead others to faith in Him, and they were not even accused of any political motives. The books which were read in court were produced to prove their apostacy from the Roman Catholic Church and her doctrines, and French, English, and Italian Bibles were quoted in their accusation. All tended both to show the reality and the simplicity of their faith, and also to publish the truth.

I send you a letter written by Rosa Madiai to her husband, after the trial, and before the sentence had been pronounced. It will be found to be a striking instance of the grace of our Lord in answer to prayer, when the state of the poor sufferer is remembered, and the depth of her feeling of disappointment two months ago, when her trial was off. Yours, affectionately, D. K.

LETTER XVII.

Rosa Madiai to her Husband.

Mio caro Madiai.—Tusai, se to ti ho sempre amato, ma quanto più ti devo amare, ora che siamo stati insieme alla battaglia del gran Rè, e che siamo stati abbattuti ma non vinti! Io spero che, per il merito di Gesù, Iddio Padre abbia accettata la nostra testimonianza, e che ci darà la grazia di poter bere fino all' ultima goccia la pozione di quel calice amaro che ci è preparato con rendimenti di grazie.

Mio buon Madiai! La vita nostra, che è? Un giorno, un giorno di dolore! ieri giovani, oggi vecchi! ma pero noi possiamo dire col vecchio Simeone, "Ora, Signore, rimandi il tuo servitore in pace, poscia che gli occhi nostri hanno veduta la tua salvazione."

Coraggio, mio caro; poichè noi conosciamo per lo Spirito Sano che quel Cristo carico di obbrobrio, calpestrati ed inguiriate, è il nostro Salvatore, e noi per la sua santa luce e potenza ci troviamo a difendere la santa croce e Cristo spirante per noi, ricevando i suoi obbrobri per noi partecipare della sua santa gloria. Non teme se la condanna sarà forte. Dio che fece cadere la catena a Pietro e aprivala porta della sua prigione non dimenticherà ne anche noi.

Sta di buon animo; rimettiamoci intieramente in Dio; fammetti vedere lieto, come spero per la medesima grazia mi vedrai lieta.

Ti abbraccia di cuore
La tua affezionata moglie,
ROSA MADIAI.

Questa lettera è stata scritta dalla Madiai in carcere il di 7 Giugno, 1852, quando il pubblico Ministro aveva già concluso perchè fosse condannata, come poi fu condannata alla pene di 46 mese di Ergastolo, e il marito ai 56 mesi di casa di forza e pubblici lavori.

(*Translation.*)

She encourages him; our ground of confidence in God.

My dear Madiai.—Thou knowest how I have always loved thee; how much more, then, must I love thee now, that we have been together in the battle of the Great King, and that we have been cast down, but not vanquished. I hope that through the merits of Jesus, God the Father has accepted our testimony, and that He will give us grace to be able to drink, even to the last drop, the bitter cup which is prepared for us, and that, too, with thanksgiving.

My good Madiai; our life—what is it? A day, a day of grief; yesterday, young; to day, old; but, nevertheless, we can say with old Simeon—"Now lettest thou thy servant depart in peace, since *our* eyes have seen thy salvation."

Courage, my beloved; since we know, by the Holy Ghost, that *that* Christ who was laden with reproach, trodden under foot, and despised, is our Saviour, and by his holy light and power we find ourselves set to defend his holy cross—and Christ dying for us, we receiving his reproaches, that we may afterwards partake of his holy glory. Do not fear, if our condemnation be severe; God, who caused the chains to fall from Peter and opened the gate of his prison, will not forget even us.

Be of good courage; let us cast ourselves entirely into the hands of God; let me see thee joyful, as I hope, through the same grace, thou wilt see me joyful. With all her heart embraces thee,

Thy affectionate wife,

ROSA MADIAI.

This letter was written by La Madiai, in prison, June 7, 1852, when the public minister had already determined that she should be condemned, as she afterwards was condemned, to the penalty of 46 months of the *Ergastolo;* and her husband to 56 months of *Casa di forza* and public works.

LETTER XVIII.

Rosa Madiai's dejection of spirits; cheered after awhile; her ill health.—Maggiorani's application to the Minister of Justice.—The appeal to the Court of Cassation.—22d: Hopes that a fresh trial at Lucca may be ordered.—24th: Contrast between the Florentine rejoicings, at "the feast of St. John," and the condition of the imprisoned.

FLORENCE, June 18, 1852.

MY DEAR L.—My last letter contained an account of the trial, and the very severe sentence passed upon Francesco and Rosa Madiai. You must have observed that remarkable self-possession she exhibited in court, and in what a truly Christian spirit she wrote that beautiful letter to her husband;

she was afterwards sadly cast down, and lost patience for a short time. Truly we hold this treasure in earthen vessels, that the excellency may be of God. Her kind lawyer and friend, who had power to see her, succeeded in comforting her after a time, and in a few days she had recovered her usual calm resignation. We must remember how very weak poor Rosa is in health, and what an effect continued solitude has on minds—in some cases even inducing insanity; and then we must also remember how very vexatious to a nervous temperament must have been the constant disappointments to which she had been subjected; so that, perhaps, our wonder should rather be, that she had been enabled so constantly to exhibit such submission, and not only so, but such an ardent desire to glorify God in her sufferings.

On the 12th poor Rosa was very unwell, and suffering from fever and nervous excitement; she was told that a petition would immediately be presented for a commutation of the sentence, and also of a notice of appeal to the Court of Cassation. Francesco was marvellously strengthened; his only desire was, that the will of God should be accomplished in him—he was in perfect peace; poor Rosa, through extreme weakness of the flesh in nervous agitation, did not enjoy this rest. On the 15th she had still much fever and loss of appetite, but had great unity of spirit with her husband. It was hoped that they might have the consolation of seeing some Christian friends, indeed it was promised, but upon application for admittance it was peremptorily refused; I heard, however, that one friend had been permitted to see them occasionally.

Yesterday Maggiorani saw the minister of justice for an answer to the petition for grace; the reply was very tersely given. The case must first go to the Court of Cassation, and after the result of that appeal was known, the petition will be considered; but without any pledge as to the nature of the reply. It must take at least a month before the appeal can be made, so that the prisoners are at once subjected to this extension of imprisonment, with all its uncertainties. I trust that God will, in His infinite mercy, sustain and comfort them in this fresh trial.

22nd. They say now, the result of the appeal cannot be known until the 21st of July; if the iniquitous sentence to which they have been doomed should be broken, a fresh trial will take place at Lucca, and there appears to be a good hope of a favorable result. The Lord has sustained Francesco in uninterrupted peace; he says he has given himself up entirely into the hands of God, that He may do what He will with him, and to Him he entirely leaves his destiny; he was glad to suffer for the Lord; he had read, he said, that thus the Lord has always led his children through persecutions, and was it not the very religion for which he suffered that made him so happy?

the only grief he had was to think of his dear wife's sufferings.

* * * * *

24th. To-night there will be fire-works in honor of St. John,* and all will be apparently festivity and joy; and yet, in the jails of this very city, shut up in close narrow cells, are some dear to Jesus, suffering for His name's sake.

Yours, affectionately, D. K.

LETTER XIX.

Publication of Maggiorani's defence; interest expressed about it.—Bicchierai's speech against the Madiai published.—His admissions in favor of the character of the accused.

FLORENCE, July 6, 1852.

MY DEAR L.— * * Maggiorani's admirable defence has been published; it has made much stir among all classes. Even the Grand Duke has read it. Many quite unknown to the author have written to him, complimenting him in strong and feeling terms upon his able and classical defence of the Madiai. Some of these letters are from the first lawyers of the Tuscan bar. Landucci forbade advertisements of it at the corners of the streets, but it

* St. John the Baptist is the Patron Saint of Florence; his festival occurs on Midsummer-day.

has been advertised in all the papers except the *Monitore*, which refused to insert it. Copies have been sent to various places; I hope you will soon get one.

Bicchierai has published his speech against the accused. It commences with a sort of laudation of the Madonna. One remarkable admission he makes, "that although the Madiai's witnesses have proved their *natural probity*, their *beneficence*, kindness and charity, that this only made him the more regret their having left the Church, and did not make their crime the less. What a noble testimony, from their bitter persecutor, in their favor!

Yours, affectionately, D. K.

LETTER XX.

The case heard before the Court of Appeal.—The judges apparently favorable.—August 7. The former sentence confirmed.—The Leopoldine Laws set aside.—A petition to the Grand Duke prepared.—The tried condition of the prisoners.

FLORENCE, July 31, 1852.

MY DEAR L.— * * The Court of Appeal has heard the case of the Madiai this morning. Maggiorani, as usual, spoke remarkably well, and was listened to with the most intense interest by all the court, who seemed to be much better disposed towards the accused than the former court had been; and there is but little doubt *now* that they will find for an appeal, and then the matter will be heard over again at Lucca; and *most* likely the court will consider their past imprisonment as sufficient, and ask for their discharge. Oh, what a mercy it will be, should they be set free; we must still hope in the Lord. If it is His will to deliver, He will deliver; if not, He will give more grace to endure. I will not send this letter until I hear the ultimate decision, so farewell for the present.

August 7th.—Alas! all our hopes have been dashed to the ground. This morning the Supreme Court rejected the appeal made to it, to set aside the sentence pending against the Madiai. All the legal men agree in opinion that this refusal to hear the case over again is as usual, first, against the evidence adduced against the Madiai, which evidence cannot on any grounds condemn them; second, that in confirming the sentence of the first court, they, like it, violate the true interpretation of the Leopoldine Laws.* This court, therefore, enforces in every par-

* The Leopoldine Laws take their name from Peter Leopold, (or Leopold I.) Grand Duke of Tuscany, from 1765 to 1790. His reforms in the criminal and civil administrations of justice were alike remarkable. "In his new code, the criminal section was especially bold, inasmuch as it swept away at once torture, confiscation, secret trial, and even the punishment of death. * * * All privi-

ticular the first sentence; so you see that no court of law in this country is free and independent; for, instead of being expounders of the law, they are rather interpreters of the will and wishes of the government, who wish that the case of the Madiai should serve as a precedent for any other similar case which may come before them, so that all may know what to expect.

Maggiorani has prepared another petition, which will be presented immediately to the Grand Duke, and it is the opinion of all that it will be granted. Nevertheless, in all probability the government will allow both the Madiai to be carried to their different prisons, and after keeping them there a couple of

leged jurisdictions were destroyed, and the public courts fortified in their independence and authority. * * * * Leopold's ecclesiastical reforms were equally daring, and gave deep offence to the Papal government. * * * HE SUPPRESSED THE INQUISITION; he imposed severe limitations on the profession of monks and nuns," &c.—*Spalding's Italy*, ii. p. 307.

On the death of the Emperor, Joseph II. in 1790, his brother, Peter Leopold, succeeded him as Leopold II. bestowing the Grand Duchy of Tuscany on his second son, Ferdinand III. who was the father of the present Grand Duke, Leopold II. who succeeded in 1824.

The general tenor of the Leopoldine Laws was to confer on the Tuscans personal and ecclesiastical freedom of action, and to render *public* all the proceedings of government.

Where are now the Leopoldine liberties? Even if there be *pensieri liberi, parole strette* must accompany them!

weeks, will then commute their punishment into perpetual exile, and thus show how tender and considerate they are in the midst of victory. It is a question, in my mind, whether either of the Madiai will be able physically to bear the first shock of a removal to the galleys. They will no longer believe in a commutation, because their hopes have been so often frustrated. But the Lord is able to help—"My grace is sufficient for thee;" and His promises are able to lift them above all circumstances and pain, notwithstanding that the flesh is so extremely weak through long and wearisome imprisonment. Let us pray that the poor Madiai may "hope in God, who raiseth the dead," and rejoice in a certain resurrection. When the result of the petition is known I will write to you again. Maggiorani has shown himself extremely kind and feeling throughout this long affair. I must now close this letter.

Yours, affectionately, D. K.

LETTER XXI.

H. M—y to N—— and L——.

Rejection of the petition for grace.—Visit to Francesco Madiai in the Murate prison; his submission and message to his wife.—Visit to Rosa in the Bargello; her sufferings; her prayer.—Her removal to Lucca.—Her message to her friends.—Husband and wife not allowed to meet since their trial.

FLORENCE, August 10, 1852.

MY DEAR FRIENDS:—The petition for grace was peremptorily rejected! This summary proceeding, which allowed no opportunity for the interference of the Prussian or English minister, was known to a few on Monday. Maggiorani, their lawyer, was absent at Leghorn, and did not hear of it till Tuesday, when he immediately returned here. We went together to the Murate prison; Madiai was in perfect peace; he received the final blow in a spirit of holy submission, and the only expression of suffering was, squeezing my hand, saying, "There is need of patience," but cheerfulness beamed in his countenance, although suffering from continual physical illness. He also said, "The comfort and joy of the Holy Spirit never changes with me; however it may be with my poor body, I am always happy; God has been with me all the time of my imprisonment, and He will always be with me as long as I remain in prison, and I am as sure that He will be with me unto death." He wished to have with him a supply of clean linen, &c. adding, "If permitted;" we found on inquiry, that *this was not permitted;* he instantly smiled, saying, "Well, all things according to the will of God." He talked beautifully about his wife, and requested me to tell her that his prayer was that God would go with them to their prisons, and that he felt sure that God would be their companion there. I have seen Christians die in perfect peace and happiness, but I have never seen so complete a triumph in the midst of life, the will in the sweetest accordance with the Divine will, the whole man following Jesus in the simplicity and gentleness of a new born infant, and at the same time with the dignity of a man!

Afterwards we went to the Bargello: her sufferings were great, but they speedily assumed the character of Christian fortitude. She at once took leave of the various topics of hopes and fears, which had long kept her noble spirit in painful exercise, and turned to her stronghold. "Tell all, not to pray for our liberation, but for that increase of faith which may enable us to suffer cheerfully." And then, before us all and the attendants, she burst forth into fervent prayer, especially for more faith, more love to Jesus! The doctor was in the prison at the time, she sent for him; I was much pleased with him; and although it was unusual, he said he could give her a certificate as to the state of her health, requiring diet different from that of the common prisoners, as absolutely important to her life. We remained an hour with her. Maggiorani has fixed to go to Lucca to see that everything is provided that can be permitted, and perhaps I may go also.

This morning early I received a most unexpected notice from one of the prison officers, that she was going off instantly, and wished to see me. I filled a small basket with tea, sugar, &c. When I arrived at the Bargello, K—— very kindly let me go to her cell. I found her meeting this trying moment most nobly. She explained to me that she wanted her bonnet, gown, shawl, &c. these were under the care of W——. I soon brought them. She asked me to leave her for a few moments, when she quickly dressed, and appeared smiling. She said, "I have done nothing to my hair, for they will cut it off." She sent much love to you all, and so did he, mentioning you by name; she said with much feeling, "Remember me to all the brethren, and tell them, should they be called to follow us, to bear what may be appointed them to suffer, but never to forsake their God! I desire not only to take up the Cross, but to bear it cheerfully with abounding thanksgiving. What an honor it is for such unworthy creatures to be called to suffer in the Lord's cause." I handed her into the carriage, and we parted under a great blessing; she was attended by a female jailer and some gensdarmes. I can give you no account of his departure to Volterra; no doubt he is gone. What barbarity, thus to separate husband and wife, who have never met since their trial. I can make no comment.

Your sincere friend, H. M——Y.

LETTER XXII.

H. E—— to F. D——n.

Remembrances of visits to the Madiai.—Francesco almost always composed and happy, resigned to the will of God: his firmness in his Evangelical profession.—Agitated at a false deposition against his wife; his deep feeling for her. —Left in his cell while unlocked; effect of the stillness of the prison on his nervous system.—Mass in prison on Festas.—The prayers of the Madiai for their enemies.—Rosa's inferior health and nervous temperament; occasional despondency; contrition of spirit; sustained by faith.—Anguish at the sufferings around her.

FOLKESTONE, Sept. 4, 1852.

MY DEAR FRIEND,—Finding that Miss W—— had sent away her copy of Francesco's letter,* I have again translated it for you; it is, in my opinion, a precious document now, showing in Madiai's own

* Inserted above; Letter XIII. This letter from H. E. was written in answer to an application for a copy of Francesco's letter, to be inserted in this series of extracts.

simple, truthful way, his growth in grace, and in the knowledge and love of his Saviour. We think that you may like to have some of our well-remembered conversations with our dear Madiai; we may, but I do not think we do, put an undue value upon them. Make what use you like of the information I give you; interweave parts, or all, or omit it altogether in your pamphlet of extracts from D. K.'s letters, as you think best; but I cannot but believe, that having this information from those who had heard such noble professions from the lips of the prisoners, would give an additional interest and force to the perusal of your work, should it fall into the hands of the incredulous and the scoffer, having had your information from those whose high privilege it had been to visit these noble Christians in their prisons, and who had beheld with wonder and admiration the sustaining power of grace and simple faith, evinced by the holy submission of those dear prisoners. I will write the different circumstances as I remember them, without amplification or comment; the truth, the simple truth, and nothing but the truth, do I communicate to you.

With one exception, we always found Francesco Madiai perfectly composed and happy: unmoved by the hopes and fears of his friends respecting his ultimate fate, he ever calmly and sweetly expressed "his entire resignation to the will of God in all things." He once said, "I desire to be as a lamb in His hands, to do with me whatsoever seemeth to Him good." When some one remarked, that perhaps the authorities were detaining him long in prison in order to induce him to recant, he answered warmly, "I abjure my faith and deny my Saviour? who, even in my bonds makes me so happy! Never! They may do what they please with this poor body of mine; I may, perhaps, die in prison, but, with God's help, I will never deny Him; and what I say for myself, I am as sure of for my poor wife, who, weak and ill as she is in health, is firmer than myself in faith; well do I know this." The only time when we saw him agitated and unhappy, was after having heard that a false witness had deposed that his wife had, on one occasion, taken from her her rosary and had flung it into the Piazza; he grieved lest any one should believe that his wife was capable of committing so violent and unseemly an action. He used sometimes to say, "I should be a stock, or a stone, were I not to feel my imprisonment and separation from my wife and friends; I do feel it deeply, sometimes, but still God makes me so very happy, that, were it not for my poor wife I should be content to remain here. Sometimes, indeed, the devil (il Maligno) comes to tempt me to despond; when he does so I rise instantly, and rapidly walk up and down my cell, repeating my psalms, and then praying earnestly to my Saviour for help, and soon do I become calm and happier than before."

Very beautiful and very affecting was it to see him sometimes with clasped hands, and up-turned tearful eyes, praise and thank his merciful Saviour for all his great kindness to him, a miserable sinner, and then repeating with much emotion his favorite 116th and 51st Psalms.

One day he told us that, the lock of his cell door having been broken, his jailers were consulting where to place him, whilst it was being sent to be repaired, as the prison was so full there was no adjacent vacant cell; "Leave me where I am; were every door in the prison open, I promise you I would not go out of it until I had been tried, and I had made my public confession." "And so they did leave me," he said, laughingly. When his friends told him that they had in vain endeavoured to obtain leave to see him more frequently, he said, smiling, "I am very grateful for all your kindness, and it is a great pleasure to see you; but still, I confess, that if I had never seen any one, I am sure I should have been happy, for my good Saviour is ever present to comfort me."

His demeanor towards his jailors was most gentle and courteous; he was always unwilling to occupy his chair until they also were accommodated. He sensibly felt the terrible silence and stillness of his last prison, the Murate, where he passed six months in solitary confinement previous to his trial; he said, "It was the silence of the tomb," no sound of clock or bell reached him. He asked, as a favour, to have his watch returned to him, "as a companion;" it was refused, and he patiently bore his disappointment. The window of his cell was built up, convent fashion, so as to admit light and air, but to exclude all view of the outer, living world. Happy as he ever was, it was painful to see his physical, nervous derangement, in the twitchings of the face, and the trembling of his hands; still was he more than conqueror, through Christ strengthening him.

It appears that on *Festas*, mass was performed in the prison chapel; during which the door of every cell was opened half-way, so as to permit each prisoner to see the altar. When asked what he did on such occasions, Madiai answered, "I retire to the furthest end of my cell, and repeat my psalms, and pray." During all his trials and sufferings, no anger, no bitterness did he express against his persecutors. Neither Madiai, nor his wife, ever uttered a word of disaffection, or of disloyalty; on the contrary, they frequently prayed for their enemies, that it might please God to touch their hearts and to open their eyes to the truth, before it was too late.

Poor Rosa's broken health, and highly nervous and sensitive temperament, caused her to feel her sufferings and trials more acutely, and sometimes she temporarily gave way to despondency and fear; and deeply touching it was to witness her deep and humble contrition for her occasional lack of faith. "Oh, how unlike am I to St. Paul! I ought, but do not, *always rejoice in tribulation*, and never to faint, but the spirit is indeed willing, though the flesh is very, very weak; oh! pray for me that my faith may increase." And truly, her faith enabled her to make as bold and noble a confession as did her more constantly rejoicing husband. When told of her husband's firmness and happy state of mind, she exclaimed, "Oh! what good tidings are these, better, far better to me than would be the possession of any worldly good." One of her great trials was in seeing the anguish and misery of her fellow-captives, and being unable to aid them; this, to her compassionate and tender nature, was a grievous sorrow. She was often, during the nights, roused from her slumbers by the moans of newly arrived prisoners, whom they were conducting to their cells; and for several successive nights she was distressed by the screams and violence of a female prisoner, next door, who was accused of murder. Such were some of our dear prisoners' trials; happy pri soners!—

"They who to the end endure
The Cross, shall wear the Crown!"

Ever your affectionate, H. E.

REPORT OF THE TRIAL.

From the *Gazzetta dei Tribunale*, Florence, 12th June, 1852.

ROYAL COURT OF FLORENCE.

Camera Criminale decidente, sitting of 4th June, 1852. President, Counsellor of State Signor Nicoli Nervini; Public Minister, Proc. Gen. A. Bicchierai; Counsels for the defence, A. Maggiorani and R. Tenici.

TRIAL OF MADIAI.—IMPIETY.

Not having been able to assist at the debate on this interesting cause, as it was held, by request of the Public Minister, with closed doors, we hasten to publish the act of accusation and the sentence.

ACT OF ACCUSATION.

The Royal Procurator-General to the Royal Court of Florence, deposeth:

That the Chamber of Accusation (*Camera d' accusa*) of the Royal Court aforesaid, by a decree set forth 25th November last, has ordered that Francesco and Rosa Madiai, husband and wife, and Pasquale Casacci, be accused of the Crime of IMPIETY.

In compliance with this decree, the undersigned having examined the regular instructions compiled in the tribunal of the first instance, of Florence, declares that from the same substantially results what follows:—

As regards the Madiai, there has existed here for some time, and, unhappily, it has been sought to propagate amongst us, a heterodox confession, called "The Evangelical religion, or religion of the pure Gospel," which, refusing in many points the Roman Catholic faith and discipline, and substituting private judgment concerning the knowledge and interpretation of the Scriptures for the authority and traditions of the Church, impiously attempts to displace from the minds of the believers the pure and healthful principles of Catholicism, and to put in their stead false and condemned doctrines, to increase the number of its followers, and to enlarge its boundaries, to the insult and prejudice of our most holy religion, and the civil ordinances on which this rests.

To this confession belong Francesco and Rosa Madiai; who, not content with having apostatized from Catholicism, in which they were born and brought up, have even sought to disseminate and insinuate in others their errors, without regard to age, sex, or condition, and directing this wicked propaganda against the weakest and least experienced, placed, also, under their authority.

It is likewise ascertained that they lent their dwelling for the convenience of reunions, both for religious exercises and for the instruction of the members, particularly after these meetings were put down in other localities; that such a reunion was held on the 17th of August last, when the public force discovered it, and made arrests and perquisitions; that at various times books, tracts, and heterodox works were deposited and kept there, and afterwards distributed by *decurioni;* that, at the said reunions for instruction, many came, even more than twenty Catholics, (not excluding children,) some of whom thus imbibed and were confirmed in the errors of their sect, and that the Madiais, even out of this reunion, profited by every favorable occasion to exercise proselytism, preaching and insinuating, amongst other things, maxims contrary to the sacrament of confession, to the real presence in the Holy Eucharist, to the sacrifice of the Mass, to the doctrine of Purgatory, to the worship of the Sacred Image, to the intercession of the Blessed Virgin and the Saints to the Priesthood, to the Pontificate, to the observance of certain feast-days, to the forbidding of certain food, &c. They also distributed Bibles, translated, and not approved by the Church, and books of prayers corresponding with the errors mentioned.

Some persons declare that they refused to join, in spite of repeated insistance; others, that they incurred the risk of falling; and one (Antonietta Marsini, their servant,) confessed that she indeed fell into error, so far as to partake twice of the Communion that they celebrate in commemoration of the Last Supper, and to follow in some things Rosa Madiai, who urged her to break the beads of her rosary and the scapulary she had on her neck, as being objects of idolatry.

The Madiais confess to their apostacy, and deny the proselytizing, but admit having taught the truth to those who sought it from them. They are contradicted in this by not a few witnesses.

In consequence, Francesco, son of the late Vincenzio Madiai, 48 years old, married, without children, native of Diaceto, in the prefecture of Pontassiene, living in Florence, a courier, and letter of lodgings; and

Rosa, daughter of the late Stefano Pulini, wife of the said Madiai, native of Rome, living in Florence, aged 50;

Are accused of impiety, committed by the above mentioned individuals in the course of last year; and particularly by the Madiai, workers of a propaganda and proselytism to the so-called Evangelical Confession, or the Religion of the Pure Gospel, not so much by teaching as by the distribution of books and tracts, to the prejudice and insult of the Catholic Religion predominating in the Grand Duchy; a crime foreseen and punishable by the 60th article of the law of 30th November, 1786, and by judicial observances.

Written at the office of the Royal Procurator-General, at the Royal Court of Florence, 6th December, 1851.

A. Becciuerai, Royal Proc. Gen.

Speech of the Public Minister, Sign. A. Bicchierai.

I have the honor of again speaking in your presence, in a cause grave, extraordinary, and delicate, and on this account necessary to be noticed, as opportune and in its juridical position.

I should never have believed that our office would have needed to hear accusations in defence of the religion of the state in this country, where every memorial, every building, every institution, every object of art—I would almost say, where even the very stone and cement speak to the mind, and the heart of all, of that august daughter of Heaven, under whose wings the country and people of Tuscany have become illustrious, respected and envied.

Still less should I have believed it, after that the so-called civil progress had shown itself pending and inclining before Her, almost to attain to that *consecration,* which is alone worthy to accredit and give strength to innovations, and great and splendid undertakings.

Still less should I have feared to recognise in the enemy's ranks any sons of this same religion, after the extravagances of the fanatic, Jean Souchott, afterwards passing into England, and thence to America and Switzerland; divided and subdivided into many more branches and twigs, all working with most impotent means to diffuse and spread abroad Bibles adulterated, mutilated, or changed according to their fancy, and without authorized commentaries, in every spoken language, and even in Italian, permitting every one to read, comment upon, and understand it according to his own private judgment, or the explanations of anti-Catholic ministers.

The Romish Church has made head against them as it could, by authority and instruction, by recording and reviving the discipline and prohibitions of the Council of Trent, and the provisions of Benedict XIV. Thus did Pius VII. Leo XII. Pius VIII. and more particularly Gregory XVI. in the encyclical letter of 8th May, 1844, written explicitly to condemn the Society of the Christian Alliance, which was instituted at New-York in 1843.

Of this encyclical letter, (referred to in Cappelletti's History,) the following quotation is worthy of notice:—"It is clear, and proved by a long experience of past times, that to draw the people from fidelity and obedience to their princes, there is no method so easy as that indifference to religion which the sectaries propagate under the name of religious liberty. Nor do the new members of the Christian Alliance deny this, for though they profess themselves averse to exciting civil seditions, they nevertheless confess that, by giving the multitude the right of interpreting the Scriptures, and thus diffusing among the Italians what they call total liberty of conscience, the political liberty of Italy will, spontaneously, arise therefrom."

These words are an anticipated comment on the events of our time. Civil liberty being extended, and time being given to constitutional systems, as if by the consent of these, the dissenting or Protestant confessions, transformed and with various titles, though identical in substance, emerged from their hiding-places, or poured forth from America, Switzerland and England, into Italy and Tuscany, and worked hand in hand; not so much to establish themselves for the private benefit of their followers, as to propagate their principles by gaining proselytes even from the Catholics. And when the Italian governments were in the height of disorder and of internal revolt, we saw this propaganda increase in numbers and boldness; for to those who studied to pervert by means of religious sects, the political agitators joined themselves, and alternately gave and received help from the others; thus both parties proceeded, their ends not always the same, their means also different, but producing and working the same effect, doing harm to the morals and religion of the State, and thus to public order, on which society rests. Hence impious public preaching, which you condemned in the parish-priest Barni; hence the offences against the Catholic religion and the pontificate by means of the press, which you repeatedly punished both in the journals and in the printers; hence other singular acts of impiety, also repressed by penal justice.

But the work most hidden, though extensive, and most destructive precisely, because so hidden and carried on insidiously, is that of the Heterodox sect called the Evangelical Confession, or of the Pure Gospel, and sometimes also called the Brethren. This could not be efficaciously laid hold on, notwithstanding the many cares, attempts and measures adopted by government to get at it, and although it was well known to be much extended in Florence and in other towns, as well as in the country.

It was only on Sunday evening, the 17th August, 1851, that this was accomplished, by means of access and arrests at the house of the accused, Madiai, followed up by the regular instructions which opened the way to this trial.

Speaking now on this matter, and it being my duty to sum up the results, and present them before you, I must premise that of direct political elements, the cause of the Madiai offers no trace. They figure in it solely for the religious element, and for the consequences thus produced upon public order. You will soon, indeed, have to know and judge another affair, already passed to the *stadio difensionale*, in which both elements are combined, and where that of religion figures only as a means to political disturbance. We cannot, however, affirm, nor do we allege, that the Madiai knowingly worked as the instruments or organs of a political sect. The facts objected against them by the accusation were directed to themselves, and considered in their nature and religious tendency; but in this end, and in these facts, exists in reality the crime of attacks upon the religion of the State, and it is therefore indirectly political.

This mode of expressing ourselves will clearly show the spirit understood to be given, and which will be maintained with regard to the accusation. No; penal justice is not so rash or foolish as to presume to avenge the offended Majesty of God. And when we hasten to the defence of the religion of the State, we consider Catholicism not as what it is in itself and its relations with God, but as it regards the advantages which it renders to public order and to society, which entertains, venerates, and favors it as a fundamental necessity of its institution.

The intrinsic dogma of the *infallibility* of its nature and essence, while it does not permit one to suspect that the *rock* will ever shake, nor that the *doctrine* which rests upon it will diminish by one iota, yet is not a warrant or assurance that it will be permanent in our countries. This doctrine does not support that idea, and history proves the contrary. Therefore, the protection and defence which penal justice affords is not to it nor for it, by means of it to the country and to society; and thus it is a defence of the State, of its order, its existence and prosperity.

Far hence, then, be every apprehension, every anxiety which—not in your minds, but in those of others less experienced—might give rise to inopportune fear or exaggerate wicked comments. The present cause was not originated, nor was it fed, by indiscreet and intolerant religious zeal. The criminal acts of others gave rise to it, political necessity required it, our duty demanded it.

But not for this have we exceeded, nor shall we exceed by a single line, pure legality. We venerate, (and who would not do so?) equally with any one, individual liberty of conscience, as an internal sanctuary which cannot be violated by civil authority without the risk of disturbing the human race.

We respect religious tolerance so far as the guardian laws consent thereto, so far as is compatible with civil good order; and this is tantamount to saying, so long as tolerance exists, so long as it does not degenerate into lisence or indifference, whence would arise that confusion, that clashing of different beliefs, which would end in the most deplorable civil disorder.

But what, it will be urged, are the limits marked out by the laws of the country for religious toleration? You, gentlemen, will fix them in the sentence. We will without further delay trace them out.

The Madiai were Catholics by birth, by education, and by many years' profession. They lately apostatized to join the Evangelical Confession, and this they professed inwardly, and also externally in the private meetings of their co-religionists here in Tuscany, and more particularly in Florence.

But for apostacy from Catholicism, neither the accusation nor our tribunal has made nor does make any reproaches. Neither is the private profession of the new faith imputed to them as a crime, although substantiated by an exterior act, perhaps, of some notoriety; because the law was placed under the necessity either to leave unpunished such an act, although connected with an innovation of a bad precedent, and therefore dangerous—or to render illusory individual liberty of conscience by hindering those who unfortunately changed their faith from those external acts and practices, private indeed, but necessary to satisfy the requirements of the worship embraced; the law of the country, I say, has thought it prudent and discreet to pass over the first, rather than the second inconveniency.

In this they are more liberal than many writers of worth, and certainly not intolerant, (such as Cremani and Forte,) who, in the profession of a heterodox faith by one previously a Catholic, considered an external act to constitute a real crime, punishable by the tribunals of the State where Catholicism is predominant. They are likewise more condescending than legislation, much more modern, particularly the penal code of Sardinia of 1839, which would have sanctioned the same principle in the articles 164 and 165, according to what the lawyer Negroni observes, in his treatise "On Ecclesiastical Jurisdiction in Criminal Cases, &c." printed at Novara in 1843, § 22 to 24.

Let us proceed, gentlemen, to the 6th article of the law of the 5th July, 1782, and to the 6th and 7th articles of the other law of the 30th October, 1784, and from these combined, (not modified in this respect, as concerns the laity, by the articles agreed with Rome 25th April, 1851,) it will be easy to gather that apostacy, heresy and schism, as long as they are the individual defection of the Catholic citizen, cannot be judged and punished in a general way as real crimes; and that the most that can be done in similar cases is by admonitions and other ecclesiastical recalls, and afterwards by imploring the secular power as a precaution to send them into exile, lest contact with the erring should corrupt the good.

In this sense must be understood Poggi's "Elem. Jurisp. Crim. lib." 2 § 27, 32 and 34, where he admits exile against the apostate, the heretic and the schismatic.

But valuable to all are the remarks of "Carmigiani, Jur. Crim. elem. tom. 2 § 715." "It is necessary that a Catholic prince diligently protect the holy religion of our Fathers. But as we should blush to speak without having the right to do so. There is no appointed punishment in our constitution against heretics, apostates and schismatics; it is sufficient, if they only exist and have been proved to be obstinately attached to their errors, that they be banished from the State, lest they should corrupt others by their persuasions or example."

And I add, (from a complete exposition of Tuscan legislation,) that the same project of our penal code, now pending in examination, proceeds in article 159, upon the same premises, *i. e.* not to admit under the category of crimes simple and individual, apostacy and heresy; and there have been given the reasons for this in the relative report printed *a. c.* 97 *e. segg.*

But though we do not prosecute the Madiai for apostacy from Catholicism or their own personal profession of the Evangelical Confession, we cannot say the same of their acts and efforts directed to spreading among others the same errors, to propagate in a Catholic country, and to the prejudice of Catholicism, this anti-Catholic confession.

When dissent in religion proceeds from personal individuality, and is declared externally with a view to the corruption of others, or by assuming the character of proselytism, all writers, even the most tolerant and liberal, (except, perhaps, those who have been, or are, the voice of revolution,) agree in recognizing it as a crime. In such a case, the religion of the State suffers from an attack on itself and its professors; public order is disturbed by it, and society would compromise itself if it left such an act unnoticed and unpunished. The individual cannot then complain of restricted liberty of conscience, of invasion of the secrets of his belief, nor of coercion on his thoughts. It is not an evil of the mind, but a voluntary delinquency manifested in an external act, that we oppose: it is against the evil which the seductive efforts would propagate, that we place a barrier: it is for the defence of others that we provide.

And here really lies, and very reasonably, the difference between the religion of the State and the other professions which are tolerated there; since, while one should and does favor the diffusion of the former, (as Cremani observes, and after him, the above-mentioned report supplemental to the new penal code,) to the other professions is permitted its private exercise to those who belong to it; but it is forbidden them to form a propaganda, or engage in the work of proselytizing, as this is not necessary to the maintenance and free profession of one's own convictions and the peculiar principles of one's faith.

We will now proceed to the authorities, and begin at the source. After the peace given to the

Church by Constantine, and after the Catholic was pronounced to be the religion of the State, (*l. cunctos populos cod. de suum trinil,*) the Emperors Theodosius and Valentinian, in the *l. eum quis cod. de apostat,* thus expressed themselves:—"We find it good to punish by death and confiscation of property, him who by service, persuasion, or by constrained advice, has passed from the worship of the Christian religion to any of those infamous sects or rites."

"If a Jew persuades a Christian to embrace his religion, he shall be proscribed, and suffer the punishment of death."

Descending to periods less remote, we may remark that Ferdinand, the third Medicean Grand Duke, when on the 10th June, 1593, he granted the well-know privileges to the Jews and others not Christians, to attract them to Leghorn and Pisa, took the precaution to declare, article 20, that "you must not dare to attempt in any way to *persuade* any Christian to join your ritual, and in case of such action we desire that you be punished severely, *in conformity with the laws.*"

I omit the historical fact of the Huguenots, not accepted to people the Maremme, and that of cemeteries and chapels so lately conceded to Protestants within the Grand Duchy for their private religious services, although these also prove the care always taken by the Prince and Government of Tuscany to defend the country from heterodox proselytism. I return to the writer on Criminal Law. Cremoni, § 15, expresses himself thus:

"The Catholic prince has always been careful that those who oppose themselves to Catholicism should exercise themselves in their own religion in private only; and that they should do it without harm, he made them embrace the abjured religion, or Catholic, in public. He had also other rights, to prevent them from being easily seduced by those who are abandoned to errors.

"But if the guilty person dares to preach apostacy among us, and does not blush to join himself to a party, he shall undoubtedly undergo the punishment appointed by our law against other impious persons, the enemies of society."

Forti admits the same principle, *Istiting*, *Civ. art.* 115: "If an unhappy creature, having had the misfortune to be born in a place where the divine light of the Gospel had not shed its rays, persists in the error of a false belief; if others, though born in the bosom of the true religion, lose their way in the holy doctrine taught by the Redeemer, proclaimed by the Councils, and acknowledged by the Church, to enter the road to perdition, falsely persuaded that this will lead him to the gates of salvation; or if he unhappily nourishes in his thoughts some other abominable impiety, but, notwithstanding this, respects outwardly the public religion and public worship, does not outrage the general belief, and does not seek to diffuse in others his errors for the purpose of finding companions in iniquity, or to become the apostle of unbelief,—society cannot have recourse to those punishments which refer to the external actions of man, and consequently cannot apply to merely internal faults. The law cannot exalt itself to be the supreme director of consciences, nor has it the right to arm itself to constrain them to the true faith; by so doing, it would put itself in opposition to the maxims of that same august religion that it desires to protect, and far from removing impiety and errors, and preventing public scandals, would operate, perhaps, more widely to diffuse them, and would occasion, by the punishment, those evils which the guilt itself would not cause.

"Punishments are but evils, to which recourse must only be had in cases absolutely necessary to obviate greater evils. Hence the principal faults connected with religious belief, when they do not degenerate into proselytism, being faults only of the mind, can only be corrected by means tending to enlighten the mind, instead of those directed to coerce the will," &c.

And this principle is sanctioned for us in the 60th article of the law of 30th of November, 1786, and by the existing Legislation that explains it.

Article 60. "Whoever with impious intent dares to profane the divine mysteries, by violently disturbing the sacred functions or otherwise committing public impiety, and whoever teaches publicly maxims contrary to our holy religion," &c.

Here, every one will feel, three hypotheses are contemplated:

1. The profanation or disturbance of the divine mysteries *(turbatio saciorum)*.

2. The act of public impiety.

3. Public teaching of maxims contrary to the Catholic religion.

But with regard to the three categories, as well as to the *publicity* inherent in the *impious act* of the second, and the *false teaching* of the third case, it is known how civil law, urged by the necessity of not recognising defects in the law, or to supply them with common right, has fixed and always observed, amongst others, the following two canons:

1. That the publicity above referred to occurs when the act has been directed to *not less than three persons*, although not on purpose gathered together.

2. That even should publicity be absolutely wanting, the crime would not therefore cease, but would be punished with a less hard penalty than that of forced labour, (now the Ergastolo,) as it should be remembered that the 60th article of the law of 1786 does not *precisely* define the limits of the crime against the religion of the state; but rather indicates *demonstratively* to what one should

have recourse for the purpose of measuring the imputation and the penalty; and that for the definition and circumscription of the crime, one must recur to the public right, modifying and applying the penalty with the spirit of the law just quoted, of 1786.

I do not cite particular authorities with which all are acquainted, and which you, gentlemen, have often examined and applied in the last two years. The resolution in the case of Manfredini, in 1804, may suffice for all.

Neither do I fear that that will be maintained which was mentioned before the Council Chamber by the honorable defender of the Madiai, namely, that the fundamental statute of 1848, not yet abolished at the period of the crime in question, enlarging the circle of toleration, and giving liberty to every belief, rendered almost *impossible* under its dominion the crime of *religious proselytism.*

No: the condition of Tuscany was, in this respect, under the statute what it had been before, and what it has now returned to be. If the statute did not declare, conformably with the law of 1st of May, 1814, that the Roman Catholic and Apostolic was the dominant religion, at least it called it "The only religion of the State; "and the other religions are spoken of in the following terms: "The other professions now existing are permitted conformably with the laws." This permission, thus subordinate conformably to the existing laws, proves evidently that all the principles of law and jurisprudence, till then put forth, remained in full vigour; and it was so much the more necessary to respect them, that the dangers to be avoided for the religion of the State were increased, by enlarging civil liberty, and admitting all the citizens to the public employments.

Besides, it would be quite unreasonable to pretend that this liberty opened the way to such great and lax toleration, since every one might have said, done, and preached, or at least taught in matters of religion, whatever they pleased to the Catholics. Knowledge of such a fact would of necessity have led to latitudinarianism, and thus have cancelled the first words of the statute, that it was founded *only* on Catholicism.

Too many, both here and elsewhere, have, in fact, shown that they understood it in the former manner, because that suited them; but this was license, not liberty, not rectitude but calumny, not right but crime. And one should be answerable for this.

Gentlemen, I have endeavoured thus far to explain, with doctrinal and reasonable deductions, all that in history or right seemed to me strictly necessary clearly to dispose, appreciate, and resolve on the present cause. I will now come nearer the case itself, and speak of Francesco and Rosa Madiai.

The act of accusation, already known, dispenses with the necessity of making a long exposition of the elementary facts which are there collected, and I believe, with truth, precision, and without exaggeration.

The results of the trial seem to me to have verified and explained them, as much as was necessary not only for legal, but moral conviction.

I mention particularly the entire, irrefragable depositions of Antonietta Marsini and Antonia Zaccagnini, which are very full upon all the charges brought to bear not only on Madiai, but also on his wife. Their modes of deposition, the coincidence between them in many circumstances, as well as in other depositions and in the documents: the fact that they could have had no interest to lie or calumniate, powerfully speaks in their favor, and recommend them to your justice and conscience. I cannot admit any valid objections against belief in their testimony. If there appear to be any, they are hazarded with respect to the woman Madiai, but all irrelevant, inconclusive, and not verified, nor capable of being verified. These depositions suffice, in my opinion, to decide in favor of the accusation.

We may, nevertheless, also take into account the frequent discussions of Vecchioni, either with Madiai or his wife, in which they inculcated false and impious principles, intending "to turn aside her also," so that for this reason she ceased to work in their service. Nor must we overlook the depositions of Bucciolini with regard to the wicked insinuations of Madame Madiai, and the doubts of the above-mentioned Marsini and Zaccagnini at an unsuspected period.

We may also add, with regard to Francesco Madiai, the depositions of Guiseppe Centofonti, Guiseppe Cavaciocchi, Serafino Vannini, and Enrico Matterassi.

From the declarations of the witnesses above-named, it is proved that the Madiai gave accommodation in their house to the Evangelical reunions, not only for the exercise and confirmation of the converts, but also for instruction for others, for the most part Florentines of low extraction, and Catholics, and also little children, who should have been sustained and brought up in Catholicism. That these were generally gathered together in the evening, and sometimes in the day, and that a certain Malan, an Evangelical minister, came there to teach those initiated, but not yet admitted to communion, and after he was banished from Florence, others came in his stead and performed his part.

It has been proved that in this house they received, kept, and distributed, personally, and by means of *decurione*, books and tracts of the Evangelical sect, printed in London, Florence, or elsewhere; that this distribution in the town and country was not made by Madiai alone, but also by his wife (as well as others,) who sometimes rejoiced, at the increase of brethren, and the recent success of the propaganda, compared with the preceding sterility. Among the said books were the Bible in the Italian of Diodati, and prayer-books of the Protestant sects, which were given to Zaccagnini and Marsini, and sold for a small sum. also to Materassi and Centofanti, as well as to others not known.

It has been proved that the Madiai (who had hung up in a room a small print quite opposed to Catholicism) did not lose opportunities to instruct in, and draw to, their creed even Catholics, by ridiculing and throwing discredit on the fundamental principles of the Catholic dogma, and substituting others of their sect. The act of accusation sums up the principal errors by them inculcated, which are many and diverse. All have been proved by the depositions of the witnesses, and they may also be proved by the so-called articles of religion in the said book of Protestant prayers given to Marsini by Madame Madiai. These errors, and this impiety, cannot be classed as such without the judgment of the Church. But as they consist in the elementary principles, it will be sufficient to refer, as was done in the case of Barni, to the most obvious and elementary opinions of the Christian doctrine, as well as to the rules and discipline of the Council of Trent. I will not pause to make the comparison, for fear of further wearying the court, but I can assure you that there is no error mentioned in the act of accusation which has not been condemned by a canon of the said Council, or other earlier œcumenical Councils.

It has been proved, finally, that the woman Zaccagnini was much loosened from her Catholic convictions by the plausible address of Madame Madiai, and perhaps, also, by the benefits she bestowed or procured for them from others; and Marsini was still more disturbed, and was induced by the insinuations of Madame Madiai to dispense with scapularies and rosaries, and was induced twice to partake (as they say) of the communion; it signifying little that the first time she did it of her own will, blinded by the corruption of her mind, caused by the teaching of the said woman Madiai.

In these facts, it seems to me, there is proof of entire and consummate impiety, of proselytism, which, I repeat, ought to be considered as *impiety of act*, resulting, that is, from single or diverse acts, in which oral teaching only constitutes one part, and which, therefore, will fall under the second rather than under the third category (though this a matter of indifference) of crimes in the 60th article of the law quoted of 1786.

Neither is it necessary to recur to the aid of the

jurisprudence as far as regards *publicity*, since the teaching has been secretly diffused, and given or procured individually, or almost individually. That did not consist merely in oral teaching of anti-Catholic doctrines, if we duly appreciate the depositions of the oft-mentioned Zaccagnini and Marsini.

But leaving this, and proceeding with the criterion of regarding proselytism as an ascertained fact, resulting from many and diverse individual facts, it is easy to arrive at the fact of *publicity*, and not only that real, actual, *effectual*, which would, indeed, be sufficient as far as regards the natural inevitable consequence of the act, but also that *inherent* to the act itself, and thus part or portion of the same.

The repeated admission to the domestic conferences of many people, (sometimes above thirty, often more than ten, latterly only, in consequence of the increased risk incurred on account of the greater vigilance of the Government, reduced in number to four or five,) this repeated and frequent admission, I say, of many people, not yet all separated from Catholicism, but on the way to separation, and to perfect or confirm themselves in the evil; the convenience and aid afforded to the distribution of books and tracts calculated to lead astray, are facts which plainly and truly indicate publicity, and which cannot be separated from this without destroying them. In this sense, and with these same causes, does Raffaelli understand publicity in his *Nomatesia Penale*, quoted and reported by *Roberti Diritto Penale*, tom. iv., art. 53; the said Roberti likewise understands it in this sense, and thus, also, the Sardinian penal code, cit. art. 164, recognising it in the dispatch or distribution of books, or other printed works attacking religion, as well as in public teaching or public harangues. (*V. Negroni*, toc. cit. sec. 22.)

For the rest, it was public and notorious that there existed a confession of the pure Gospel; public and notorious that this was directed against Catholicism, and loudly and unweariedly declared against certain legislative and Government measures; public and notorious that the Madiai belonged to the said confession; finally, public and notorious (and this is to the point) that they took part efficaciously and heartily in the propagation of the false doctrine, in the distribution of wicked books; so that the priest of their parish felt himself compelled to make a report of it to the episcopal authority, to be enabled to provide a remedy, as it treated really of doctrine. Thus publicity in the sense and for the requirements of the law was not wanting; on the contrary, it was great, therefore scandalous and highly hurtful.

Of the guilty intention, I do not think a question can arise. It is inherent in the criminal fact.

Whoever works the Protestant propaganda, to the prejudice of Catholicism, intends and desires that this should fall, and that prevail. No one would proselytize without desiring to do harm to the object against which he wars. This appears clear to me, and this exhausts the formal reality of the crime. The analogous terms, if you choose, may be seen in the learned observations of the "Ruota Criminale," in the celebrated cause of sacrilege and falsity, against the priest Borsini, concluded by the decision of 14th May, 1831.—*Relatore Bologna.*

I will not expatiate on the depositions of the witnesses, called in favor of the Madiai, and particularly of Rosa.* They appear to me quite irrelevant to the cause. Most of them apply to a period previous to that in which Madame Madiai declares to have decidedly and really abandoned the Catholic communion, to join the Evangelical; and all those who speak of acts of respect to the articles of religion, to the sacraments, priests, saints, undoubtedly refer to a time previous to that included in the present cause. None of them, besides, relates facts

* The advocate then entered on a long argument in favor of Rosa Madiai, on the plea that she had, on various occasions, as declared by the witnesses, acted as though she had still been of the Romish church. This was done in order to prove that she did not openly insult the Roman Catholic religion. We do not undertake to defend his line of argument.—*Trans.*

which destroy or shake those of the accusation. That to a priest and Catholic curè, conducted into their house by a relation, the Madiai should even in 1851 show themselves as Catholics, and not tempt to convert him, was but too natural, and I will say necessary, as well as prudent, particularly at a time when the Government operations had, in many ways, and on many occasions, shown themselves against the work of their sect. The same will hold good with respect to what Rosa did before a person who, at another time, had seen her maintain the part of a good Catholic, at the bedside of an infirm and dying woman.

The acts of goodness, natural probity, and benevolence, that Madame Madiai wished to urge in arrest of judgment, may cause one to grieve more over her separation from Catholicism, but cannot free her from the present crime and accusation, nor diminish the imputation cast upon her.

To estimate this, one must, I think, take into account the more aggravated evil, that the Madiai were Catholics, and the greater scandal that this circumstance produced and maintains, and their obstinacy, which does not decrease, but rather gains strength in the face of the special government and legislative measures.

Neither do I think that after these measures, particularly after the law of the 25th April, 1851, and the condemnation, in consequence, of Count Guicciardini, of Betti and others, their co-religionists, one can speak of the good faith of the Madiai, or of their having any doubts as to the nature of what they did cautiously and with reserve, plainly showing their consciousness of not being permitted to do so.

Things being in this position, the case of the Madiai offers, if I mistake not, all that weight of criminality for which the 60th article of the law of 1786 desires, that such crimes be punished "with the utmost rigor, and never with a less penalty than of forced labor;" which had, and still has, means to apply itself to the greatest as well as to the least degrees of crime. I do not propose a difference between the two accused, because their guilt appears to me equal, considered thus in the lawful facts of harm, as in the formal reality of action.

In the case of Buletti, (decided 7th August, 1851,) you fixed the term of imprisonment at thirteen months; in that of Messeri, (decided the 13th of the same month,) you ordered the same punishment for a year. But in these cases the impiety consisted in single and isolated facts of contempt for the sacred image; scandalous facts, undoubtedly, but such, however, while they show the depravity of mind, and irreligion of the agents, as do not so easily disturb the faith of others, nor bear a hostile attack on the religion of the state, being in their nature disagreeable and repulsive. The crime of the Madiai, politically considered, in itself and in the means employed, is much graver and more hurtful than those. I do not think I shall exaggerate, however, if I make my final request for one of the inferior degrees of exemplary punishment.

Defence of the Accused, by the Sign. Odvardo Maggiorani.

"In matters of religion we ought to avoid the use of the penal laws. It is true that these laws cause fear: but since religion has its own penal laws, which also cause fear, one must be conquered by the other." Placed between these two, the minds of men become ferocious.

Religion has great threatenings, and, at the same time, great promises; so that when these are present to our mind, "whatever may be done by the udge to make us abandon our religion, it seems as though he leave us nothing if he take that away, and that he takes away nothing if he leave us that."*

These solemn words of Montesquieu sum up all the questions which I shall propose to you. They are at the same time the conclusion and the commencement of the weighty arguments by which I desire to be able to prove to you, that society has nothing to hope from judicial inquisitions, but rather

* Montesquieu, de l'Esprit des Lois, liv. xxv. ch. 12.

everything to fear, if it is attempted, by means of these, to arrest the progress of heterodox ideas.

Such proof would not be without its value. It would seem to me opportune, when, for the first time in these halls is sounded an accusation of *proselytism*, and the wise custom is broken which banished from our law the sanction of this crime. It would seem to me opportune, when you and I (indeed who does not see it?) are witnesses of the interest taken in this judgment by the public conscience, which, a short time ago, had not even a suspicion that the bases of civil and religious society were undermined, and which now stands in apprehension lest the already enormous weight of our political calamities, if not added to, should be aggravated by a question which of itself alone, (I will not say where the fault lies,) has sufficed to desolate, for many centuries, the greater part of the Christian world. The public mind had not foreseen this misfortune at which to-day it feels so troubled. Not long ago it openly applauded a great genius* who, treating of the political question, proclaimed that Italy could never become Protestant; and this applause, if it was a homage rendered to truth, should have been worth, as a guarantee, that no one would be hardy enough to lend a hand to the rash undertaking. This unusual cry of the accusation fills with sudden terror the ignorant city, which cannot per

* Gioberti, del Primato morale e civile degl' Italiani.

suade itself that its religion can have so suddenly been placed in so much danger, that the disturbance of a trial can be preferable to that generous and intrepid toleration which, in our public right, is almost traditional.

The novelty of the accusation, however, the public fear, the harm which is certain to arise from this judgment would persuade me to discourse, at some length, on the great questions summed up in the words of the ancient President of the Parliament of Bourdeaux. But I am not of such long standing, neither is this the place to discuss that which appertains to a merely moral order, unless it reflects directly on the judicial question.

To define, by its extremes, the crime of *proselytism*—to inquire if these extremes are to be found in the facts objected against the accused—to show the invalidity or irrelevance of these facts: such is the office to which it is necessary that I confine myself.

And I announce it to you, now: but that I may propose to you an exact definition of the *title*, I must premise, with some considerations, which are of use to separate it from what does not belong to it. You and I ought to determine the crime of *proselytism* by the guidance of our civil and penal laws: to separate from this cause all that regards a different and superior order, and which might easily be confused in our researches. To this I confine myself, examining what are the relations of these laws with religious matters.

Liberty of conscience, the toleration of all religious opinions, these great fundamental principles of our public right, are those which rule the question. Political reasons, civil reasons, economical reasons, moral or Christian reasons, all concur in guaranteeing its inviolability.

The state represents, in the political order, society such as it is, in its reality, in its internal divisions, with its intellectual and moral dissensions. Its purpose is to assure to all men, whatever the differences that separate them, those conditions of their intellectual, moral, religious or material development, which the conscience of each one has judged preferable. Even the atheist, according to Filangieri, has a right to social protection. According to others, to him alone may this protection be denied, because atheism is not a religious doctrine, and the State need not lend it any succor: secondly, every man ought to be free to profess the religion which best pleases him, but one he ought to profess, and there is no religion without the eternal principle of God. Therefore, every religion has a right to be tolerated by the state, which abandons error to the fate reserved for it, that is, to be destroyed by the progressive knowledge of the truth.

And that which is in the nature of the state is also for its best interests. Since sound policy requires that men should not be provoked to violation of the law, nor to martyrdom; and whoever acts otherwise, may be called as imprudent, as inhuman.

And if it is important to society that every individual should have a religion, what can it augur from him who should be obliged to profess to have one, to which his conscience cannot lend itself?

More than this: material punishment inflicted by the state exalts the error, and confers upon it an importance which, perhaps, it has not: irritates the mind, invites retaliation, and renders legitimate, in some manner, civil war.

To these political reasons may be added civil ones. Since the first possession of man is that of the thoughts and conscience, a possession free and inviolable, a faculty which cannot be coerced, upon which God himself acts by the grace and light of truth. "If the origin of social power should be derived from the tacit or presumed consent of the people, it is easy to prove that it could never have been the intention of any man to limit personal liberty, beyond what was necessary for the preservation and advancement of the social condition."* Hence one could not, without invading the most sacred of possessions, impose on the human conscience a religion distasteful to it.

* Forti, ist. civ. lib, 2 cap, 2 § 56.

In the third place, we have economical reasons: since there cannot be material prosperity in a state where religious intolerance makes of a part of the citizens, and sometimes the most considerable, a class of persons unrecognized, denies them the benefits of the common law, interdicts them public offices, degrades in them the moral sense, and clips the wings of all noble aspirations. This, besides being an enormous injustice, is a political error. It is an in justice, because if you except the atheist or him who professes a religion of depraved morality, every dissenter may not only nourish, but constantly exercise most scrupulously, the maxims of honesty and uprightness. It is a political error, because, if no one can deny that religion, as an internal sanction of the truth, is one of the greatest guarantees for the good of society, then it is likewise certain that, considered in this point of view of social utility, it satisfies the civil wants of men under whatever form of worship, and with whatever dogmatical doctrine. True it is that one ought not to participate in the errors of others; but society ought not to expel others from her midst because they hold different convictions. "One ought not to hate him who errs on account of the error, nor love the error on account of love to him who errs."* History warns us how, in former times, the economical conditions of

* Greg. I. 43.

society were extremely deteriorated where intolerance flourished, whereas they were wonderfully advantaged where the contrary principle was carried out. The Republic of Venice, compared with the rest of Italy, and still more strikingly with the other nations at that struggling epoch, proves this truth.*

But even if all these, and many other reasons, failed to persuade one that the principle of liberty of conscience and religious toleration should be respected, Christian morality would yet plead for it, and the interests of religion, in the name of which primitive justice is invoked.

"The morality of the Gospel was announced to the nations as a law of charity. According to the Apostle Paul, charity enlivens faith, and holds the first place among the Christian virtues. This charity embraces all the human race, comprehending Christians and infidels, righteous and sinners. The difference of faith does not free one from the natural obligations of humanity, nor from the civil obligations imposed by the law, or arising from convention. The Christian ought to hate the sin, flee from the dangers to which the sinner might expose him; but cannot, by reason of the sin, cease to consider as a man him whom he knows to be guilty. To those who err, should be given counsels, admonitions, and fraternal correction; but they cannot be put beyond

* Darn, Hist. de Venise.

the law of humanity. This doctrine, derived from the purest fountains, was taught even in those times when practice seemed most to contradict it. Those very laws which conceded unbounded lisence towards the persons of the heretics, nevertheless supposed that they acted without hatred or without personal rancor, almost as delegates of the public authority. * * * Human life is a time of grace and hope, nor can man, who is ignorant of the mysteries of Divine Providence, take upon himself to decide if his brother, who lives in error, may not in time render the most splendid testimony to the truth. * * * To punish error with temporal penalties, is to anticipate Divine justice, and almost to despair of truth. Persecution renders the persecuted more obstinate; gives the consolation of the affections to their opinions; cuts short the road to mature reflection, and multiplies the moral impediments to repentance. Hence it appears that the practice of seeking out the private opinion of individuals, and making it an article of crime, is opposed to the good of religion. The distinction between the internal and external forum is essential not only to civil, but to ecclesiastical laws." *

Droz, after having said that he hopes never more to see persecutions nor religious wars, and that this century may not end before the work of re-union

* Forti, loc. cit.

already attempted by Bossuet is undertaken again, adds: "To prepare the way for that union which will fill heaven and earth with joy, let us show ourselves always just, affectionate, ready to do service to our deluded brethren. Much is done towards the union of mind when hearts are brought near together. They know not how much harm they do who exaggerate Catholic principles, and thus, without intending it, alter the Word of God. They terrify minds which need encouragement; their bitter language drives back those who would walk towards them, while the voice of charity produces effects very different."*

If to these reflections you would add the authority of the Church, you will find as much as you can desire.

St. Gregory, in the most unhappy times of Christianity, denominates tyrannical the punishments inflicted on heretics, since the misfortune which is a consequence of the fault seemed to him sufficient punishment. He says there are evils which cannot be cured by punishment, but must be tolerated. And even the Apostolic Constitutions contain this teaching, said to be of St. Ambrose.†

* Droz, pensieri sul cristianesimo, e prove d'ella sua verita—versione italiana del padre Tanzini § 27.

† Greg. ii. 34; v. 2; xii 24 xi. 46. Conct. ap. vi. 23. Ambr. ep. 82. Greg. xiii. 2.

In another place, after having inculcated that Dissenters should not be driven back with violence, Gregory adds, that whoever acts differently, shows that he has at heart his own cause more than that of God.

* * * * *

With these maxims, and to this teaching, fact does not always accord. Let us cover with a black veil those monuments of the ferocity which dared to call itself the keeper and vindicator of the Gospel. We should regulate our actions by the divine law, and not by human passions; and the divine law cannot be more explicit.

The Apostolic Constitutions declare that it was forbidden to every bishop, priest, or deacon to speak to the unbelievers, or to force them to change their religion. Chrysostom teaches that one ought not to recall Christians from error by coercion and violence, because against error no other force is given to Christians but that of the word; and if this does not avail, all is lost.

These are the rules of Christian morals, which make liberty of conscience and religious toleration a necessary, inviolable principle. Sound philosophy had indicated this before the light of revelation shone on the human mind. Cicero had proclaimed that religion cannot be preserved by violence and fear, but by those relations with which man binds himself to God.

And conformably to these maxims we find the Fathers of the Church to have acted. Indeed more than once St. Gregory gave a safe conduct to the heretics, to take away every suspicion that he wished to use violence; which proves that he had the power to punish, but did not choose to make use of it. And St. Ilario prayed the emperor to permit the people to choose freely their masters, and bitterly lamented that the church would constrain people to the faith by exiles and prisons, almost accusing of weakness that Christ, whose name they make a cloak for their own ambition.

I will not go on seeking the many examples I could adduce to prove to you that civil persecution never succeeded in extirpating heresies, but rather taught how they might be maliciously propagated. If you glance at the history of the first centuries of the Christian era, down to modern times, you will find sufficient to persuade you of this. From the time of the Goths who, under Theodoric brought Arianism among us, down to the errors of Hermes and Ronge, what has not been done to extirpate Anti-Catholic creeds? Still we have never succeeded, and the occasion for heresy, given by St. Paul,* has now received the seal of nineteen centuries.

To one single example will I refer, to prove that

* 1 Cor. xi. 19. "For there must also be heresies among you, that they which are approved may be made manifest among you."

only with mildness and counsel it has been possible in some places to obtain what processes and condemnations did not procure in the greater part of the world. The blood of the Huguenots inundated, for two months, in the sixteenth century, the whole of France. Was heresy conquered? Civil war arose more tremendous than ever, and in 1598 was promulgated the edict of Nantes, which secured to the Protestants the exercise of their worship, and the rights of citizens. Such was the last result of the massacre that rendered memorable the fearful night of St. Bartholomew.

In one place only the horrid carnage was not executed. Jean Hennuyer, Bishop of Lisieux, opposed all the force of his authority and his character to the royal lieutenant who communicated to him his barbarous mission; and the Huguenots of Lisieux were saved. And Maimbourg, in his History of Calvanism, states that in this place alone were the Huguenots persuaded to abandon their faith.*

Reason, science, experience, history, all support the authority of the principle of liberty of conscience and religious toleration. Let not the words appear idle which I have spent on these arguments; they bear directly on the interests of the defence. Vattle † says it is a shame to humanity that a truth of this

* Maimbourg Hist du Calvinism, liv. vi. page 355-358.

† Le droit des gens. liv. 1 § 127.

nature needs to be proved. He says this, however, after having clearly demonstrated it. For there is no principle, be it ever so true and clear, which ought not to be amply demonstrated when it is destined to exert a powerful influence on the case in question.

Applying this principle with that system of elimination which ought to lead us to circumscribe, in its true terms, the idea of the crime of proselytism, it is quite clear that there cannot now be question of apostacy nor of heresy in the civil tribunals. Our laws, indeed, which, particularly after the reform of 1786, were inspired by the principle of toleration of the celebrated treaty of Westphalia, do not make mention of these crimes. Roman, or anterior legislation relative to these, have certainly no weight with us now. The Grand Duke Pietro Leopoldo, who decreed punishment for *public impiety*, excludes, by omitting from the list of crimes, heresy and apostacy, which, as they only offend against God, ought to be judged and repressed by God, and not by man.

Apostacy and heresy are not then among our list of crimes. The principle of liberty of conscience and religious toleration assures us the power of modifying or changing our belief. The laws do not oppose themselves to the free exercise of this faculty.

All this proceeds upon the foundation, that human justice ought not to make itself the vindicator of outraged divinity, nor arrogate to itself the rash office of searching into the secret relations between man and God. While man neglects the duties which he has as a man, towards God, society cannot interfere. Instead of being an act of justice and faith, it would rather be one of pride and unbelief: it would be appearing to consider one's own strength greater than the Divine power.

But every man has also his duties as a citizen; and the same principle of liberty of conscience and religious toleration which is his right, forces also an obligation upon him—that of respecting in others the exercise of the same right. Therefore, every time that he neglects this obligation, which is altogether civil, he commits a crime against society, and it is then that human justice can place him under the penal laws.

This, then, is what determines the action of these laws: SOCIAL EVIL A CONSEQUENCE OF CIVIL GUILT.

This distinction did not escape Pagan policy, and much less that of the Christians.

The Republic of Rome repressed the Bacchantes and the Druids, but for political and not religious reasons. The Bacchantes put in danger the security of the people and government, and corrupted morality. The dispersion of the Druids was necessary to secure to Rome the dominion of Wales and Britain. Cicero, Valentinian, Adrian, &c. all agree that none should be condemned for profession of Christianity, but should only be interfered with when their machinations harmed the empire, or when they were guilty of civil crime.

Such likewise is the doctrine of our most celebrated authorities; Cremani, Nani, Poggi, &c. declare that man cannot punish those evils which offend God, unless they are prejudicial to public order or the tranquillity of the State.

Let us now examine the crime of proselytism.

As crimes are imputed politically, not on account of their natural pravity, but for the harm they render to civil society, it follows that the crimes of religion cannot be imputed, except as contrary to social order; and therefore should be distinguished by the extremes of acts politically prejudicial.

1. External action;

2. Direct intention to overthrow or suppress religion;

3. Publicity or public scandal.

Here it would be superfluous to bring forward doctrines, for our laws could not be more clear and precise.

The 60th Article of the Reform of 30th November, 1786, contains evidently all the theory that we have premised: "Whosoever with impious designs dares to profane the divine mysteries, disturbing the sacred functions *with violence*, or otherwise commits *public* impiety; and whoever *publicly* teaches maxims contrary to our holy Catholic religion, towards which we have always nourished, and will always maintain constant our love and zeal, we wish, that as a *disturber of the order* upon which society is maintained in tranquility, and as an enemy to society itself, he shall be punished with the greatest and most exemplary rigor, nor ever with less penalty than the public forced labor, for a time or for life, according to the circumstances of the case."

The law thus requires that the action be performed with *guilty* intention, and accompanied by *publicity.* Only then can it punish, as only then it recognizes in it a civil crime.

* * * * *

Thus impiety could not be imputed to him who reasons of his heterodox belief, with others professing the same creed; nor to him who, from zeal for his own convictions, is discovered maintaining them by conversing and discussing privately with individuals to whom he is related by parentage or friendship; nor, still less, to him who, questioned concerning his belief on this or that subject of religion, replies according to his own convictions, though these be contrary to the Catholic faith, if this be the religion of the State.

Here one must reflect: how could our laws, which do not recognise a crime in apostacy or heresy, proceed so severely against the apostates or heretics as not to tolerate, that in any circumstances, or with any persons, they should manifest their belief?

It is hardly worth while to consider the case in

which the dissenter makes a profession of his principles with his co-religionists. In those countries where a religion of the State is recognized, the law may hinder dissenters from the public profession of their faith. That is to say, they cannot, without permission from the authorities, erect temples, publicly invite the faithful to their offices, or assume any public organization whatever. But if the law consent to liberty of conscience, how can it forbid them to exercise privately the worship of the religion to which they belong? One must suppose in the law an inconsistency or breach of faith, which is contrary to all rule.

Besides this, when the law forbids the inculcation of heterodox maxims, it excludes the case of teaching among persons belonging to the same communion, since this would not be teaching, but worship. This, then, is a case where there could be no question of impiety or proselytism.

Let us imagine another case. Suppose that a Calvinist is reproved by some one for not venerating the saints, not fulfilling the pascal injunction,* or that of fasting, not attending at the holy services; and if this reproof, made with acrimony and insolence, provoke the Calvinist, or at least place him under the necessity of expressing his convictions; the law, which does not blame him for belonging to that

* That is to say, at Easter, every individual Catholic Calvinist is commanded to take the Eucharist translation.

confession, can it in this case punish him because he has diffused impious doctrines, contrary to Catholicism? It would be absurd.

Society, you will agree with me, tolerates all religions, if they are not opposed to its life and progress; but in exchange for its toleration, it requires that every one have a religion, which he must sincerely profess and cultivate. Hypocrites are not less prejudicial to society than are atheists; and religious indifference keeps pace with hypocrisy and atheism. Society cannot therefore permit that submission to the dominant religion should push the heterodox person so far as to make him dissimulate his own religion or transgress the precepts which *it* enjoins.

And if the hetorodox person, to whom, by chance, an explanation is required of some Biblical passage, or some point of doctrine or moral, reply contrary to his convictions and his belief, would he not be guilty to society of that hypocrisy and that religious indifference which is so prejudicial to it?

All this seems to me strictly logical and natural. Proselytism can neither be imputed to him who communicates with his co-religionists, to him who maintains his religion against attack and outrage, nor to him who, being consulted, replies according to the religious doctrine to which he has devoted himself.

But this is not all. The principle of liberty of conscience and religious toleration, joined to the political necessity that every one have a religion which he must tenaciously and sincerely observe, leads to other consequences.

One cannot exact impossibilities; and as there is an impossible in physical order, so is there in moral order. "The law," says Nani, "cannot require from a man that which it is impossible for him to observe, from the irresistible impulse which he has by nature." And nature has given man a necessity to expand and communicate with others.

Now religion is the life of the soul, the treasure of all hope, and the supreme law of man; all created things are subordinate to this; it watches over the conscience and affections; rewards and punishes, grieves and consoles. Who can then pretend that the father or friend does not desire to share with his beloved ones, the benefits of that faith from which alone he hopes for salvation? Could the father, whom nature prompts to educate and assist his children, without failing in the most sacred obligations, direct them to a way which, in his convictions, can only lead to error? How could he inculcate in his children an idea of God, which does not correspond with that God from whom he hopes and fears everything? And is it not the same if we speak of friend or confidant? Since friendship unites two hearts into one, and institutes relationships which nature has not formed, but which she watches and seals, and, I would almost say, renders more sacred and inviolable, because they depend solely on man's choice.

The judicial idea of the crime of proselytism cannot then be enlarged; it must rather be restricted to the narrowest limits, if we would not deny that which is essential to humanity, and to the interests of civil society.

To require that the citizen should not join in the worship of his religion with his co-religionists; that he should suffer in peace, the outrage of his religious convictions, without seeking to defend them; that he should reply against his conscience by dissimulating his views, or pretending opposite convictions in presence of those who ask counsel of him; to require, finally, that he should not love to inculcate these in the minds of persons dear to him, would be to desire things at once prejudicial and impossible. You would suppose the law to be inconsistent or unfaithful; you would condemn society to tolerate hypocrisy and indifference, evils which are at the head of practical atheism; because the man, degraded and humiliated to the necessity of imposing silence on his own conscience, and externally following a faith which he does not feel in heart, becomes the most formidable and cunning enemy to every religious belief. You would pretend to the impossible, because you would seek to give the sanction of human justice greater force than that of Divine justice.

In none of these cases, in which there is an external profession of heterodox maxims, can the accusation of proselytism be propounded, since that profession is not animated by impious designs, nor the direct intention of overturning the dominant religion; an impious design or intention, *guilty intention* in fact, which science, law and jurisprudence, proclaim a necessary extreme of crime.

But the *guilty* intention does not suffice, there must also be the *evil done.* Here is another extreme necessary, in order that the judicial idea of the crime may be applied to the fact. *Affectus sine effectu ne imputetur.*

And in order that the evil may be verified, it is necessary that the means employed by the delinquent to accomplish the proposed iniquity be proportioned to the end.

I will not stay to repeat the elementary theories of criminal right. It is a common maxim of this science, that as from inopportune and feeble acts, society need fear nothing, so the law may, without danger, leave these unpunished.

* * * * *

In the crime of proselytism, the evil naturally ought to consist in that civil offence from which society suffers when its religion is subverted; in the *disturbance of public order.* And, in fact, our wise legislator ordains that the impious man be repressed only as a disturber of public order, on which society rests, and its tranquility depends. * * * Well, then, in order that *public order be disturbed,* in order that *public scandal* be produced, what is necessary? That the preaching or instruction be *public* also. Without this, there is no possibility of crime.

Publicity of teaching as the means of evil, disturbance and public scandal as an effect of the crime, these are the other two extremes of proselytism.

"If the violation of religion," says Giuliani,* "is committed in secret, and leaves no permanent trace behind it, even though it come by chance to the knowledge of one or two citizens, *publicity being wanting, the political evil would vanish also.* To make it public (note well these words) by a trial would cause more evil than advantage. Besides, to penetrate the domestic walls to bring to light such actions, would give a shock to public tranquility, would absurdly substitute the political magistracy for the pious functions of the pastors of souls, and would open the way for vexation and calumny."

Publicity has always been considered an extreme of the crime of religion. I say *always*, excepting perhaps those times in which humanity was scourged by the impious zeal of the fanatics, and impious party anger. The crime of proselytism in particular, cannot be conceived without this postulate. Let the principle be established, that only those actions can be civilly criminal which are offences against the order of the city, and the consequence naturally fol-

* Istit. di dir. Crim. lib. iv. part. 1, trat. 2, § 1.

lows that that only can be a crime in religion which is committed in a public place and in presence of the congregated public. * * * * * To go back to the Valentinian and Justinian codes, we find that they consider publicity to exist only when religious subjects are treated of to a crowd assembled and listening. The commentators, and the well-known writers of the law, Nani, Cremani, &c. all prove that impiety to be considered as a civil crime, must be committed in public. The absurdity of considering an act public when performed in the presence of three persons, is so preposterous as not to need long arguments to refute it.

Let then those maxims be no more invoked, which some magistrates sought to establish in the beginning of this century. They were an offence against the law, which you should now repair. The law was in those days violated, and much more would it be so at the present time, when the principles of liberty are receiving increasing development.

Liberty of conscience, toleration of all religions, are two cardinal doctrines of our public right. The penal law cannot meddle with certain questions without causing a wound in society greater than that which it would prevent or heal. If the crime of religion becomes a civil disturbance of public order, human justice may interfere with this disturbance. If not, *Deorum injuriæ diis curæ.**

* Tacit. Ann. i. 73.

Our laws are, thank God, formed on these three principles:—guilty intention, publicity, and evil. These are the extremes of proselytism:

Guilty intention, that is the direct intention to overthrow the religion of the state.

Publicity of the action, because without that there can arise no harm nor crime.

Evil done, an indispensable element of every crime.

Let us apply these theories to fact.

In the course of my arguments I ought now to examine if in the facts imputed to the Madiai there exists the first extreme of the crime of proselytism, *guilty intention.*

I could, indeed, omit this inquiry. Why go back to the nature of the crime, where there is not material for it? Why should I seek to discover who killed Clodius, if it is proved that Clodius is not dead?* Why the delinquent, if there is no crime? The defence might be concluded without this second inspection. Nevertheless, because the accusation has not withheld imputations, and because it is never superfluous that the defence consider even the least supported hypotheses, and finally because it is necessary that the order observed in the questions of right should be maintained in the examination of facts, I will begin by the inquiry: If the accused

* Cicero pro Milo.

ever proposed to make proselytes to their faith by means of overthrowing the religion of the state.

You see them, gentlemen: There are those apostles of heresy on whom the accusation, after having found words to denounce them to you as destructive of society, propagators of false doctrines, subverters of consciences, has also invoked upon them the severity of your judgment. You see them, you have heard them, and you can imagine how dangerous they must have been to the state.

He descended, when a youth, from the hill of Casentino, where he left his father and brothers at the plough, was domestic servant for many years to our patricians. Later, he travelled as courier with foreign families. He thus visited many parts of Europe and even America, and only from time to time remained a few hours amongst us.

Her destiny has not been different. From Rome, where she was born, she went as ladies' maid to wealthy families in England, Belgium, and Germany. She lived more than twenty years in London. Returning to Italy, she met Madiai at Florence, having known him already on the other side the Alps. They became man and wife. Her feeble health did not permit her again to attempt a wandering and troubled life. Joining her scanty savings with those of her husband, they furnished a house, and let it to foreigners, and particularly to the English, who from the wealthy and free coasts of their island, mistress of the seas, desired our balmy air and sunny sky, and who liked the ample resources which, at one time, made our civil life so happy.

Thus, neither extraordinary nor common culture, neither natural greatness of mind nor strength of soul, neither abundance of words nor the subtleties of metaphysics, neither social grade nor conspicuous position, invited them to enterprises so vast and perilous. Their only care was, by their industry to gain the means of subsistence. The wife provided for the interests of their house in Florence; the husband, who enjoyed good health, continued his wandering and precarious life, the greater part of the year in distant countries, he spent the least part by his own fireside.

Could these persons cherish in their minds the idea of overturning society? of snatching it from its belief, of throwing down the throne of Peter to place in its stead that of Calvin, of destroying the work of so many centuries, of changing the faith of our fathers? Do you believe that the Madiai meditated these things?

But they have abandoned the religion in which they were baptized; they have confessed to belong to the Evangelical communion. Thus cries the accusation, as if one must from this necessarily infer the charge of proselytism. That the Madiai should have professed the Evangelical religion, though born in the bosom of the Romish Church, cannot cause wonder, and you would not deduce from that, that they are guilty of proselytism.

It is no wonder, I say, to any one who considers their long residence in the centre of the Protestant communion. And not only have they lived in the cities of America, England, or Prussia. There they had not their own house nor their own family; no parents, brothers, or friends, with whom to stir themselves up to the observances of their own faith. They lived in the bosom of protestant families; they shared their joys and sorrows; they brought up, as was their duty, tender children to the English faith; they must often have heard the catechism of that confession; the exercise of that faith must always have been before their eyes, great were the facilities for cultivating that religion, less great than for respecting the precepts of their native faith. Less great, I say, not because the nations were guilty of intolerance, but because the rigorous exercise of their worship was incompatible with the duties they owed to their masters. Besides, attractions were not wanting which by degrees took hold on their minds. The followers of the Reform and their religion are not of depraved morality. These persons may serve as an example, whose virtues the sustainer of the accusation himself appreciated, so that in recording them, loyal and generous as he is, he was moved almost to tears, deploring more bitterly, that they should be disjoined from our Church. The

Evangelicals are Christians and rigid observers of Christian morality; and although they do not recognise the authority of Rome, and disagree with some points of doctrine, they profess all those principles which best satisfy the human heart, and best content the mind. Besides this, the quality of the persons whom the accused served, most conspicuous from lineage or education, must have caused their influence over their subordinates to have been great, and in these to have commanded obedience.

No wonder then, that they turned to another faith. If even all these arguments were vain and insufficient, who would arrogate to himself the foolish and rash pretence of searching into the secrets of their conscience? *De internis judicat Deus!*

But none can infer or conclude from this, that they designed to proselytise by overthrowing the dominant religion to which they paid always that civil obedience which the law requires. You heard, indeed, that while both the accused cultivated in secret the Evangelical faith, from the time that they were far from us, they abstained from making a formal profession of it until the force of the *civilta*, and the honest counsels of the crown introduced also in Tuscany a statute of civil franchise. Then they professed it, because all existing forms of worship were not only tolerated, but permitted amongst us,* at

* Constitutional statute of 15th Feb. 1848. Art. 1.

which time the principle of civil liberty of conscience, which was already in the spirit of our laws, was also translated and consecrated in the letter. This certainly is a proof of their submission to the civil law. They understood that no one could oblige them to believe in a certain way, but that the law could hinder them from openly separating from that communion to which the whole city belongs.

Many other proofs there are which exclude the charge made against them; and you have heard the statements of many witnesses, who declare that the Madiai uniformly respected their convictions, nor ever spoke to them abusively of the doctrines of the Romish Church.* * * * *

I must now examine the means which the Madiai are said to have employed to effect the not small undertaking of proselytism.

These may be reduced to three categories:—

1. Teaching the doctrines of the Evangelical religion to several individuals separately.
2. Diffusion of heterodox books.
3. Re-union or congregation of persons in the

* The advocate here entered on a long argument in favor of Rosa Madiai, on the plea that on various occasions, as declared by witnesses, she had acted as though she were still a Roman Catholic; the facts deposed having occurred previous to her conversion. The design of the advocate in bringing forward these acts of apparent conformity, was to prove that she had never openly insulted the Catholic religion, nor sought to make proselytes by force.

house of the accused, to exercise themselves in the reading of these books.

Let us consider the depositions of the witnesses for the prosecution.

I loudly declare that my soul revolts from descending to their infamous ranks. They expect perhaps to acquire indulgences by raising the funeral pile, and lighting the fire, to scatter to the winds the ashes of the victims of fanaticism! God himself has willed that time past should not return; and there are things which could only, perhaps, be re-produced, if former times were to return. I must however name these witnesses to you, as was my duty, and a painful one, to hear them. I am also sure that they are not men long versed in the basest acts of an ignorant and corrupt populace. We should all think that human nature would not be calumniated by having attributed to it the excesses and defects of those who are cast forth on the streets from their childhood, to grow up in idleness or beggary, father of all vices. No! I must name four women, and a youth, not yet twenty. I will not enter into the specialities of their depositions. It is enough to touch upon them, for they must appear undeserving of attention.

First, note how the greater part of these witnesses constitute, so to speak, but one body and one mind.

Enrico Materassi *has heard say* from Marsini,

that before dinner the Madiais repeated a prayer, after their own mode of thinking. He *has heard say*, from the same Marsini, that Rosa Madiai, seeking to convert her, took away her scapulary, and broke and trod on the beads of her rosary. He has besides *heard say* from Zaccaguini, *who learnt it from* Marsini, that on all fête days, at certain hours, some persons assembled in the house of the Madiai to receive instruction in Protestantism. He has finally *heard say* from Zaccaguini, that the Madiai assembled people in their house to read the Bible. This is not all, he has also *heard say*, but this time he does not recollect from whom, that they had books which they kept hid under the bed, between the mattresses, and in the cellar.

Luisa Bucciolini *has heard say* from Zaccaguini, that Rosa Madiai had given her a book. She has *heard say*, from the same Zaccaguini, *who had it as usual* from Marsini, that the Madiai had in their house re-unions of Protestants, and what not. She has finally *heard say*, and this time also from Zaccaguini, that Madame Madiai related that Teresa Petruggi had been called to the tribunal, that they made her swear upon Christ, and that that stupid creature believed it.

Does it not appear to you to be present at a phantasmagoria, and to see going round and round, alternately changing names and faces, Marsini and Zaccaguini, and Zaccaguini and Marsini? Would you not say that these two women are souls which enter into all bodies? And I will also tell you that I was deceived. I had thought them rather ignorant and unlearned, but it appears impossible that they should need to be two servants! You heard with what copious language and knowledge they recited their parts. Nor is Faustina Vecchioni less instructed. I think she might even be called "teacher of those who know."

Let us now speak of this pretended instruction. Who are the disciples of those fatal teachers of heresy? The accusation has sought them from among the known and unknown. These seven who here gave proof of such animosity and hatred to the Madiai, were not sufficient. It has made to pass across its disc a confused multitude, agitating in secret, and insinuating the fearful idea of a subterranean society.

The most odious of these pretended disciples, who have here been interrogated, is a woman:—Faustina Vecchioni. You must have remarked with what fury, worse than hostility, she has launched forth against the accused. According to her, there is no occasion in which they have not, in speaking, committed a crime; they have not exchanged a single word with her which did not horrify her. It seemed that she could not even wait for the interrogation of the judge, so great was the fury which prompted her to aggravate the melancholy condition of those unhappy people. Not only with words but with gestures and glances, she sought to instil in your mind her own fierce passions; and even when removed from your, sight she had gone to sit with the witnesses already interrogated, she did not cease her insults, more brutal than ever,—now mocking the defence of the accused, now praising the accusation.

What more? So great was her animosity that she even wished to bring forward facts exstraneous to the cause. She could not say that the accused had diffused hetorodox books. It seems that this ignorance caused her great sorrow. Therefore she went searching and re-searching her memory, and thought it a happy chance that the thought flashed across her which enabled her on this point also to bring her pious contribution to the accusation. She related that a certain Bargigli, living about a mile out of the Porta Romana, an inn-keeper, showed her in the early months of 1851, a book which had been left in his shop, by some person unknown. Having discovered that this book contained, as she said, a *confusion* of the Acts of the Apostles, (she is well versed in divinity!) she counselled Bargigli to restore it to whom it belonged, as she thought it must be prohibited. One of the reasons for considering it such, as she has declared at this trial, was that once, many years ago, she found in a cupboard of Casa Pandolfiini, a heterodox book!!!

This grossly ignorant witness only merits your contempt. The language of truth is never passionate and hostile, but cold and impartial. Who cannot keep within bounds in saying, cannot in imagining. What a difference between this witness and the accused! And I do not speak of him to whom nature has administered more strength of mind, and less sensitive feeling; but of Rosa Madiai, whose noble bearing may serve as an example as singular as rare, from that place of trial, which if it cause anguish to all, does not cause humiliation or shame.

Not only is the testimony of Vecchioni unworthy on account of its animosity, but also for the inconsistency of the deposition, and even for its falsity. It is not my intention here to discuss the religious doctrines of the Evangelical communion. I protest that as I would have desired that this trial should not take place, I will be cautious lest my words should increase the risk and scandal. But how can I refrain from pointing out facts?

And it is a fact, as Rosa Madiai affirmed, that the commandments of God are as binding on Evangelicals as on Catholics. The Evangelicals also accept the Bible, and all the Bible. The difference lies in the interpretation, and in the value set on the Pentateuch. Now, Vecchioni said that the Madiai, in reading the Decalogue, restricted the commandments to eight only. Is this true? Can it not at once be recognised as false?

She related in the second place, that Rosa Madiai denied the existence not only of Purgatory, but of Paradise and Hell. Do the Evangelicals then, not believe in Paradise and Hell? I have only to refer you to those very books used by the accusation to prove the heresy of their doctrines, and which are in your hands.

In the third place, Vecchioni told you that Rosa Madiai maintained that Jesus Christ did not die on the cross to save our souls. But do you uphold that the Madiai operated an Evangelical propaganda, or an Israelite propaganda? If Evangelical, how could she deny that doctrine which is the principal foundation of the Reform? Has not Marsini stated, having been taught by the accused, that the ceremony of the communion in both kinds is made by the Evangelicals in commemoration of the last supper partaken of by Christ Jesus before *he died for us;* and is it not an essential doctrine of their religion that our souls cannot be saved by our works, but *through the merits of the Redeemer?*

Lastly she has told you that the Madiai never named Jesus Christ, but always the Gospel. She has said it so as to infer that they did not believe in Him, or that they made Him subordinate to the Gospel. With this understanding, she has repeated it many times with that action and tone which leave no doubt of the state of her own mind. Do not the

Evangelicals then believe in Christ? Do they not believe in the Apostles? This she told you also.

Now, all that is false; you cannot give heed to it, since those depositions are not worthy of belief which affirm, (as Cremani teaches,) things impossible in their nature, or such as, considering the condition of the guilty person, and the circumstances of the case, appear improbable. And the testimony, erroneous or untruthful in part, is presumed to be so in the whole, though relating to separate things.*

* * * * *

But accepting for true all that she has narrated, can you infer from that that Madame Madiai had a school for heretical doctrines?

Vecchioni went there to work by the day. Place this woman by the side of two dissenters; make them casually meet in any place whatever—I declare to you that she would accuse them of a propaganda if they had only said a few words. Since, if she only suspected that their belief was a little less than Catholic, she would provoke them with the spirit of a Torquemada, and would put so much of bitterness with the salt of her knowledge, that they would be obliged to reply, and if they reply by a single syllable here, they are propagandists. Oh! it is not a rare thing to make people say that which they would not wish to say!

* Rot. Flor. dec. 17th Feb. 1719, cor. Beluzzi, n. 14.

The teaching of heterodox doctrines, made for the cause of proselytism, must be distinguished from academical or occasional converse. Glance at the deposition of Vecchioni. She did nothing but sustain objective conversations, now with one, now with the other. Calvin is named—one sends him to hell, the other raises him among the first. They quote Diodati's Bible, and this, for one, is an accursed book, for the other a code of religion. Is this teaching? It may be: but who holds the pulpit, and who is seeking to work a conversion? The witness or the accused? Change their places, and Vecchioni would be more guilty than Madiai.

Reflect well on the disposition of this woman—on the circumstances that I have placed before you, more particularly the one last mentioned. I do not doubt that you will reject the deposition of a witness, invalid on account of so many defects.

The second of the seven disciples of the Madiai is another servant—Antonia Zaccaguini. She also desired to forge a link for the chain of the accused. She has also confessed having long received generous bounties from them, yet has herself ministered to their sufferings. She, observe, has been three times interrogated; twice by the instructing judges of the process, once by you.

The first and second time she had not before her eyes these unhappy beings, so that she could forget she had known them. Then, frankly and quickly, (it must have been so, as the judge could not remind her of what she had to depose,) she related a long story, alleging herself the victim of a constant persecution, by which the Madiai sought to draw her away from the holy Catholic religion, to lead her to that of the Gospel. Indeed, the second time, not content with relating what directly concerned the subject under examination, she made *ultroneous*, (and therefore invalid,) statements, and began narrating how, in ascending to the hall of justice, she met a woman with a baby, who besought her to have pity on Madame Madiai, and how she had replied not to desire to deceive any one, but to speak the whole truth. Then she continued describing the appearance of the woman, and seeking by every means to draw, not only upon her, but upon all her family, the attention of justice.

Now, this witness, so zealous for the prosecution, and so well informed, how did she appear before you in this room? You saw her. She had hardly voice to make herself heard; she could not raise her eyes to the accused, nor to you. When told to turn to them, that they might hear what she with so low and trembling a voice related, she seemed nailed to her seat, and would have desired to turn her back upon the seat of the accused. Everything revealed in her, hesitation and remorse. And neither was her memory propitious, because she would have remembered nothing without the aid of the explicit and determinate interrogations of the counsellor. That she did not contradict herself was, perhaps, from fear that the court should suspect in her answers the crime of false witness.

Well might the presence of the accused render her vacillating and uncertain, since she was stung with remorse for her atrocious ingratitude. I agree that the witness must not perjure herself on account of gratitude towards the accused. The counsellor told this to Rosa Madiai when, in a moment of noble indignation, she let fall from her lips a bitter reproof. Truth, I say above all, truth and loyalty. Thus, if Zaccaguini had deposed nothing but the truth, we should only have to pity her that she was under the painful necessity of administering hemlock to one who had fed and succored her. But she has pretended and dissimulated much. She dissimulated when she withheld the fact, that if they conversed on religion with her, if they had her to read the Bible with them, if they read it to her, or presented her with one, it was because *she* asked it; because she pretended to share their faith, in order that she might more profitably draw forth their charity. She did not, however, so dissimulate, but that you could discover the truth, for, more than once, she has told you that the reason she did not break away from the net in which these evil people held her, was because of her interest in remaining with them.* These reiterated declarations ought to shed a clear light on what she has concealed in her deposition.

See, then, the ingratitude of this witness; ungrateful, not for having revealed the truth, but for having counterfeited it, and for having lied. And of her habitual fraud and dissimulation we have ample proof, so God's justice wills it, administered by herself.

Zaccaguini has told you that after having received from Rosa Madiai the Bible, translated by Diodati, and other heterodox books, she took them all to a monk, excepting one, which she burnt. Nevertheless, she continued to frequent the house of the Madiai, and to beg the aid of an ill-spent generosity. Thus, a kiss, an embrace, a feast, often cause to fall the victim of a traitor.

* She replied thus to the judge, and repeated it at the trial. She said she was only once present at the reading of the Bible made by the Evangelicals at the house of the Madiai, and that—they are her own words—" She went there expressly to see if they gave her something for her family, because she was in need, since many times they had given her something for charity; but to her, (Rosa Madia,) she found the excuse that she had gone on purpose to hear the Bible read." She added that once, to please Rosa Madiai, "because she often gave her six crazer, or a paul, or something to eat," she went to see their church. She said that when the Madiai spoke to her of the Madonna and the saints, according to the Evangelical doctrine, " she gave no heed to them, but did not let them know that."

I cannot leave this witness without begging you to meditate on one other fact to which she has referred. She related that being once in extreme need of help, she went as usual to Madame Madiai, who, having kindly given her as much as she was able, but not all that she needed, advised her to apply to the fathers of Santa Maria Novella. Zaccaguini accepted the advice, but the fathers not only refused her all assistance, but expressed their refusal with words, and in a manner, according to her, far from benevolent. In many other places Zaccaguini made the same attempt with the same success. She then returned to Madame Madiai, and so worked on her compassion by tears and entreaties that she directed her to the minister of the English church, with a note, as the witness declares, and the accused denies. This minister, after having received her in a kind manner, gave her five pauls.—See! cries the accusation, she was then in correspondence with the minister of the English church, and sent him this poor woman, the victim marked out for a wicked propaganda.

Oh, tender and faithful accusation, who could more than you smell out heresy from so far? And why from the very same fact from which you draw such sinister conclusions, may I not infer that Madiai, purposely, not to distress the timorous conscience of Zaccaguini, directed her first to the priests before she sent her to the English minister, and that she would not have sent her to him if the others had assisted her. Wouldst thou condemn her, because moved to so much pity by the complaints of that poor woman, who appeared, alas! worthy of her compassion? And if thou dost insist on believing that she recommended her to that minister with a note, what canst thou infer from that, on accusation? Was that a crime? And I do not ask thee if it would be one for Madiai evangelical, but if it would be for the most ardent Catholic?

Let us pass to the third witness for the prosecution, and she also is a servant. I speak of Antonietta Marsini. I protest that of this witness, considered of such interest to the accusation, and on account of whose illness the trial was delayed till now, I will not discourse at any length.

I will first observe that this appears to be the only person who by means of the Madiai has fallen into religious error. I say by means of the Madiai, but not even in this case is there proof of the crime of proselytism; since, to commit this crime, it is not sufficient to convert a single individual, much less their house servant.

Besides the Madiai are not responsible for the apostacy, since all that she has related is improbable, false, and therefore unworthy of attention.

She has related to you that when she first went to school to learn to read, the Madiai forbade her to take with her any of their books, or to speak of their religious belief. If that be true, no one can doubt but that the Madia used every caution to guard their secret. Let us concede more; let us suppose that conscious, of disobeying the laws, they wished to prevent the risk of Marsini revealing the practices employed by them to draw her from the Catholic faith. Well, if they were so careful of that, is it conceivable that to her, so young, inexperienced and light-minded, whom they hardly knew, they should have confided the important secret of the pretended society of brethren organized by tens and hundreds. And what other proof has there been of this pretended association, that one must at once give credence to what this woman says? It is strange indeed, that the fruitful imagination which created this new society to add to it the exterminated series of others, did not raise to the ranks of hundreds to make it at least more extensive.

What shall we say to the other insinuation of Marsini, that Rosa Madiai counselled her to break the objects of Catholic worship, that is, her rosary and scapulary? Supposing that the Evangelical Madiai, when Marsini herself had become evangelical, did tell her that these objects were signs of idolatry, since their decalogue does not permit them. Would that be a crime when the witness herself had joined the same religious communion? What would we say of a converted Turk who preserved his talismans?

You will be better able to judge of the invalidity of her statements by reflecting on what Rosa Madiai has herself said to you, and which has been confirmed by Maria della Lena, with regard to the fault committed by Marsini, and by her cruelly turned over to Madiai, namely the ceremony of the communion, of which she partook in the Evangelical Church. Rosa Madiai told you, and Maria della Lena confirmed what she said, that far from instigating Marsini to such a step, it was done spontaneously and to the surprise and grief of her mistress. She herself wished to go to the Evangelical Church attached to the Prussian legation, and then in the Via de' Serragli: and there profiting by the moment when her mistress, wrapt in her own thoughts, was withdrawing from the altar, she went there unseen by her, and to the scandal of those present.

You should also consider a circumstance only brought to light two days ago, that of Marsini's anger and rancor against her mistress for not permitting an unknown youth to come into her house, whom she wished to introduce there. I will say no more about this. May her placid dreams not be disturbed by the dark vision of the bed of grief, on which, in prison, these, her victims must lie! Can you not now conceive it possible, nay probable, that these rancorous feelings have some connection with the present accusation?

Now we come to the examination of the depositions of the other four pretended disciples of the Madiai.

With respect to the first, Luisa Bucciolini, I will premise that she cannot say that Madiai taught her heterodox maxims, since she herself admits that *once only* he spoke to her irreverently of the priest and the mass. Much less can one from this infer the crime of proselytism. "The same word," says Filangieri, "uttered in one way, raise a certain idea, uttered in another tone or with a different gesture, it wakes quite an opposite idea. How often have the most honest men been accused of irreligion, impiety and sedition, for some words misunderstood by some stupid person, ignorant of the circumstances in which they were uttered, and not distinguishing irony from the truth of expression. The fires of the Inquisition would have burnt many less, unhappy persons, if there had been less faith given to the testimonies against them."

Will you now remark the resemblance between this deposition and that of Zaccaguini? You have not forgotten that Zaccaguini took counsel with her as to the use of the books she had requested and received from the Madiai. You have not forgotten that Bucciolini has obligations, (dangerous indeed,) on the gratitude of Zaccaguini for not small sums and for signal bounties. You must finally have remarked, that Bucciolini, Zaccaguini, and Marsini, seem almost to have lent the book to each other to learn their parts. Each one of the witnesses has related her own, but all from the same drama.

You have another proof of the daring lies of this witness. She asserts having seen frequently go into the house of the Madiai, and *even a few days before their arrest*, a man whom, from her description of him, you concluded, and she agreed that it was so, to be Fedele Betti. How! Fedele Betti, who, on the 16th of May, 1851, was sent by the police for six months to Ortobello, and on the 21st of the same month, having obtained commutation of the penalty for exile elsewhere, left Florence; he on some days near the 17th of August of the same year, was again in Florence, and seen by this woman entering the house of the Madiai? Such is the ingenuity and good faith of the witnesses for the prosecution, who, wishing to oppose the *equivocal and old* facts of the depositions for the defence, by recent certain facts, and play a trick with truth, and mock the inexorable logic of the calendar.

The fifth disciple, according to the accusation, is Gurico Materassi, and he also comes to throw a stone at the head of his pretended masters. Nephew of Bucciolini, he shares with pious obedience and affection, the pilot of the three women. And this is little. He says more, in the declaration that he frankly made, that he first refused with a species of holy indignation, but afterwards requested from Madiai the Bible, which that person had, he says, shown him; and that he asked for it with the sole intention of consigning it to his mother. In a youth not yet twenty years old, such deceit and fraud cannot, it seems to me, be expiated by his determination to withdraw to a cloister. Perhaps in those sacred recesses, thinking by-and-by on past times, he will grieve over his anger and unadvised injustice towards these unhappy creatures. May he give to youths the example of repentance and amendment, as he now, alas! offers them that of a precocious malignity.

But what can be concluded from the substance of his deposition? He has related that Madiai being requested by him to teach him to read the French language, placed under his eyes a Bible translated in that tongue. He has also added the *usual* story already explained by Zaccaguini and Bucciolini with regard to the *usual* insults offered by Madiai to the priests, monks, Virgin and saints: *unum eumdemque meditatem sermonem.* Now is it credible that Madiai should have held discourses of this tenor with this youth who displays so much Catholic zeal, which he says took place at the door of the house, when he did not hold similar discourses with other people, who would have placed a better construction on them, and with whom he had quite another way of conversing, such as Giorni, Fantoni, Simoni, and so many others? This deposition proves nothing.

As to Guiseppe Cavaciocchi, and Serafini Vannini, the two last of the seven pretended disciples, recollect how doubtful both were; if they affirmed anything it was not without many contradictions, and you remained doubtful if they referred to the written examination, or if they remembered what they had said. Besides, what sort of discourses did Madiai hold with Cavaciocchi and Vannini? To one he explained some principles of his religion and his own opinions, as for example, the duty of not praying to the Virgin and saints, the too great number, according to him, of churches and priests, &c. To the other he *once* said, if I mistake not, that the oil of the light for the Madonna might have been consumed for some other purpose. Is this the teaching that can constitute the imputed crime?

But not only towards these is it pretended that the Madiai exercised the teaching of heterodox doctrines; it is said that they did so with little children. And here the accusation is destroyed by what Antonietta Marsini herself deposed. They were all the children of Evangelical parents. And if such were the case, who can reprove the Madiai for having instructed them in their religion? Can it be said that they have subverted their principles, or made proselytes, when the sovereign will of the father of the family destined them to that confession?

I think I have thus confuted one of the heads of the accusation, the *teaching* of false doctrine. For I will recall this to your minds, that to contract the crime of *proselytism*, it is not sufficient to have professed with this or that person anti-Catholic maxims, they must have been professed *with the direct intention of making proselytes, and overthrowing the religion of the State;* they must have been professed *in public to crowds assembled and listening;* they must have been *sustained in public controversy, public order must have been disturbed.*

Nor is the other head of the accusation, namely, the diffusion of heterodox books, more established. If you exclude those received by Marsini and Zaccaguini, and which cannot constitute *diffusion*, since they have been rather yielded by the Madiai than given, and since the number is too small for them to be said to be *diffused*, excluding these, whence can you conclude the said *diffusion?*

Would you conclude it from the deposition of Materassi, to whom Madiai gave a Bible that he might exercise himself in the French language, and while they stood at the house door? Has he not said that Madiai refused to give him the book when he asked for it? Will you conclude it from the deposition of the Padre Guiseppe Ricca, curate of Santa Maria Novella, who asserts that the Madiai diffused heterodox books, because *he heard say so from an English Catholic who has left Florence, and whose name he does not know*, and has also heard it from Francesco Centofanti? What authority can this witness have who only deposes *de audito*, and who, from a single word come to his ears from two persons, hastened to denounce to the Ecclesiastical Court two citizens whom he never approached, though he suspected their error, to manifest towards them those acts of pastoral solicitude which his service enjoins on him?

Let us, besides examine the deposition of Centofanti. He relates, that in 1850, having met Madiai alone at the door of his house, (it is singular that the accused so often chose that place for making a propaganda!) the latter said to him, that he would give him a book which narrated a fact that had occurred in the Low Countries, and for which book he had paid three pauls, adding, that for three pauls he had procured a true Gospel. He did not, however, give Centofanti this book, or if he did give it him in the evening, it was returned next morning without being read, for the witness, *more solite*, did not appear to have his memory very clear on that point. This, he says, he related to the Padre Ricca, and no one else; besides this, he does not know that the Madiai diffused heterodox books. Are these combined testimonies of any value?

I will not return to the depositions of Marsini and Zaccaguini, the invalidity of their evidence has been already proved. And supposing it to be true that the Madiai kept a large number in their house to distribute, may it not be believed, as the accused maintain, that they only gave them to their co-religionists? And does not this verify the *diffusion* contemplated in the penal law of 1786?

Several books and evangelical works were found in their house. Well! Have not we all, have not you yourselves, more than one serious book in your house, and more than one copy of the same book? And even of this the Madiai could have offered a plausible reason; that they had been left behind by foreigners who had lived in their house, and which they had kept because they were evangelical, or because they would have needed to restore them to their owners. In short, there is not one circumstance capable of proving this point of the accusation.

I will not discourse at any length on the third objection of the accusation, that of re-unions held at the house of the Madiai, for the purpose of reading the Bible translated by Diodati. The same witnesses who related this fact, could not omit one circumstance in which they all agree, viz: that these re-unions were composed exclusively of individuals belonging to the Evangelical confession. And when the public force, on the evening of 17th August, expected to surprise a *re-union of propagandists*, it only found there four persons: one born in the Anglican faith; two already evangelical, one for three and the other for fourteen years, the fourth, a child of evangelical parents, and brought up in the evangelical confession. Could this re-union constitute material for a crime?

Neither the teaching of heterodox doctrines, nor the diffusion of heterodox books, nor criminal re-unions, nothing is proved to justify the accusation under which these unhappy people have so long suffered.

Not teaching, because such is not the merely individual expression of anti-Catholic sentiments or opinions, and because it is not a crime when exercised towards those already joined to the heterodox communion, or who spontaneously and deliberately not wait for, but seek it; nor when it is privately exercised within the domestic walls. It is not there that they can harangue an *assembled crowd*, excite commotion or sedition among *the people;* it is not there that they dispute in *public*, to insinuate false doctrines into the *general mind.* None of these things have been done by the Madiai.

Not the diffusion of heterodox books, because such is not that small distribution which has been, if you choose to believe it, proved. It is not diffusion, because the number of books distributed was very few, and the mode of doing it not *public*, or such as to disseminate false doctrine in the minds of the *people*, (*in vulgus,*) and because diffusion is not a crime when it does not go beyond the circle of co-religionists.

Not the re-unions, or assemblies, because the heterodox do not violate the law if, in exercising the rites of a worship which the law tolerates, they retire into closer and private places, since no *scandal*, or civil *disturbance*, can arise therefrom; scandal or disturbance being facts which determine the judicial idea of crime.

Nothing of this kind is proved; and nothing could certainly be proved by means of witnesses so little worthy of attention.

But now they may rest in peace; since it has taken me so long to wake them to a sense of tardy acknowldgment of error, and it will be better for me "to leave behind me a sea so cruel."* I will only now make a contrast between the witnesses for the prosecution, and those for the defence.

The greater part of the former would have remembered nothing, if what they had before deposed had not been read to them almost word for word. I have admired the patience of the counsellor who had to interrogate them in their own words, and to awake, with studious care, their weary memories on all the particulars of their depositions. But I have also admired the supreme justice of God, when I saw those accusers, who were so bold when alone in the room of the judge, placed, to-day, face to face with the accused, lose almost their tongue and voice, pale, hesitating, deaf, forgetful and stupid.

On the contrary, how did the witnesses for the defence appear before you? Have they feared your

* "Di lasciar dietro a me mar si crudele."—Dante, Purgatorio. c. 1.

interrogations? Have they ever contradicted themselves? Did they not plainly speak the simple language of truth? And how much are they not superior to their adversaries for faith, customs, gravity, and esteem? In which do you see the integrity of face, honesty, as our wise men understood it.

I now conclude my not short discourse. I premised it with the words of one of the most celebrated writers, that the penal law can ill pretend to judge in questions of religion; and I have sought to determine when the civil power could wisely and legitimately interfere. In this disquisition I have seen fit to speak of the great principle of religious toleration and liberty of conscience. The most splendid authorities, called to the aid of reason, must have persuaded you (and surely, there was not need of so much) that this being a principle, as it is, of our political constitution, is also sacred and inviolable for the interests of all times and all societies.

Then, only, I told you, can human law meddle with religious questions, when it is necessary to guarantee the free and full exercise of that right which is a civil right; to restrain the abuse of it; to prevent others from making arms wherewith to disturb society; to restore it if disturbed.

Thus establishing the generic idea of the crime of religion civilly punishable. I have delineated the specific idea of the crime of proselytism, and have spoken of the *guilty intention*, the *evil done*, and the *publicity*.

I have examined the facts, and found that there are no proofs of the existence of these.

Not *guilty intention*, because a thousand facts adduced for the defence prove the habitual respect of the accused for the convictions of others, and because the facts brought forward for the prosecution are inconclusive and equivocal.

Not *evil* done, because no conscience has been subverted, no apprehension was caused before this trial came on, no disturbance has happened in the city.

Not *publicity*, because the accused have not preached from the pulpit, have not disputed in the cathedrals, have not harangued the crowds, nor diffused books in the public road. They exercised their faith in private meetings, in secluded places, and amongst persons already connected with their communion.

I have thus finished the defence. I have shown you the innocence of those tried. It now remains for you to pronounce their acquittal.

I have been told that the times are grave and suspicious. The pious counsel has also insinuated that I ought to abstain from defending two *unbelievers*. I declare to you that I shrunk from the base insinuation. Even if I should have run some risk I would have repelled it. The sacred office of the defence, the shield of my conscience, and the force of truth, would have rendered me fearless. But I replied with a protest, which I felt was due to all the order of the court.

The times are grave and threatening, if you will. Within here governments do not change, political faith is not cancelled. The magistracy consults the laws and its own conscience; it judges, not governs; it moderates passions, not seconds them. I do not fear for those whom I recommend to you, much less do I fear for myself. Indeed, I think that having defended them makes me worthy of your consideration.

For I did not come to implore your indulgence for the thief or murderer, who, nevertheless, have a right to be defended. I came to confute a vain and unjust accusation: an accusation that dares approach the sanctuary of the conscience, the relations of man with God, the solution of the most tremendous problem which is reserved for us after life. I came to protect two pious, upright and honest persons, if there ever was any; pious, upright, and honest, by the confession of those who have most studiously labored to bring charges against them.

I defended them with that fidelity for which I pride myself, and which at the beginning of this grave trial, the President was pleased to remind me: a fidelity which, as it ought to be a measure of the liberty of defenders, so ought to be measure of your sovereignty, magistrates.

I defended them with the full confidence which the conviction of their innocence inspired; and it is pleasing to me to repeat to them publicly the homage of my esteem and affection, now that, my office finished, I recommend them to your justice.

I feel sure you will fulfil my wishes. For within these precincts we have one only banner, one only end in our debates: for you, as for us, condemnations are defeats, acquittals are victories.

THE SENTENCE.

Sentence against Francesco, son of the late Vicenzio Madiai, and Rosa, his wife, accused of impiety.

The decree of this Court, of 25th November, 1851, having been examined, and likewise the act of accusation of the same year, the witnesses having been heard in a public discussion, the public minister having summed up, and Odvardo Maggiorani, counsel for the Madiai, with the accused themselves, having been last heard, the results of the discussion seem to be the following:—

That Francesco and Rosa Madiai, born and brought up in Catholicism, separated from it four or five years back, to embrace the religion called by them Evangelical, or religion of the pure Gospel.

That they lent their house for reunions, and when the teacher who generally presided at these was banished from Tuscany, and by means of the police this sect was broken up, and the number of those who assembled at the house of the Madiai much diminished; the meetings, nevertheless, still continued, and one was held on the 17th August, 1851, when the public force surprised three individuals there, who, together with a child of fifteen, whom the Madiai had lodged in their house for a short time, were occupied in reading the Bible, translated by Diodati, each one having a copy under his eye.

That in the house of the said Madiai were, not only many copies of the said Bible, and others in the English language, and books of prayers for the use of the heterodox, but besides, various works of the same nature, and even many copies of each.

That Francesco Madiai, profiting by the opportunity of teaching the French language to a lad of sixteen, labored, though without effect, to detach him from the Catholic faith, seeking to persuade him that it was false, and offering him, together with his wife, a prohibited copy of the Bible in French and Italian.

That, also, with others, Francesco held language insinuating that the so-called "Evangelical" religion merited preference to the Catholic belief.

That with two women who served the Madiai, and a third who lived with them about eight months, from December, 1850, they displayed the intention of leading them to abjure Catholicism, and embrace the Pure Gospel, holding with all, readings and discourses tending to throw discredit on the clergy, and the doctrines taught by them, particularly on purgatory, denying its existence; upon the holy sacrifice of the mass, declaring it an invention of the priests, and impugning the real presence in the consecrated host; upon the intercession of the blessed Virgin Mary and the saints, declaring it impossible, and dishonoring to God; upon the authority of the high pontiff, denying his power; upon the observance of other festivals than Sunday; and upon the mortification, consisting in abstaining from certain kinds of food, declaring it an invention of sinful men; upon the sacrament of communion, and upon sacramental confession, declaring the first misunderstood and wrongly administered, because it is not true the changing of the bread and wine, and because the wine ought not to be denied to the laity; and reproving the second, because made to man and not to God.

That with one of these women, older than the others, who generally maintained the discussion upon such matters, their attempts were of no effect. That with the younger, needy and very ignorant, aided with pecuniary assistance, and by continued instruction, together with books adapted to their intentions, the result was serious doubts upon the true faith. That with the third, little more than twenty years of age, and removed from all religious instruction, they succeeded in making her abandon the true religion, to adopt that professed by her masters. That the Madiai also gave themselves the trouble of teaching her to read, that she might be able to understand the books which they afterwards supplied, namely, the Bible, translated by Diodati; and another, entitled "Book of Common Prayer," printed in London, in 1848, by the "Society for the Promotion of Christian Knowledge," in which are found those maxims and doctrines condemned by the Catholic Church, which the Madiai had verbally taught, particularly that the existence of purgatory and the worship of images are foolish inventions, that in the sacrament of the eucharist there is not any transubstantiation, and other similar notorious heretical depravities above mentioned.

That the same young woman, admitted to the reading of the Bible, which they did together, commenting on it in the way already mentioned, abandoned the practice of the Catholic worship, and to obey the injunctions of Madame Madiai, who accused her of idolatry, she left off using the rosaries which she possessed, partook twice (being conducted to the place by Madame Madiai,) of the communion made by them, in commemoration of the last supper, and did not awake from her error till reconducted to her paternal house for a few days, and carrying with her the Italian Bible; this being found, caused the discovery of her wanderings.

That the Madiai denying that sectarian meetings were held at their house, acknowledge that a few friends there met together to attend to the practices of the newly-embraced religion, and declare the apostasy of the young woman in their service to have been made spontaneously by her, and not in consequence of their insinuations.

That notwithstanding this, neither their opposition nor the witnesses brought forward, have succeeded in destroying the facts objected against them in the accusation.

That Francesco has suffered imprisonment for the present procedure, from the 17th August 1851, and Rosa Madiai from the 27th of the same month and year.

Whereas, with regard to the Madiai, accused of impiety committed by means of proselytism, it appeared foreign to the question all that referred to liberty of conscience and religious toleration, because the first is not offended when the citizens are commanded to render an account merely of external acts, and the latter is guarded, not trampled upon, when it seeks to hinder others from being seduced to abandon the religion they profess.

Whereas, precisely for this, the penal laws, agreeably with the declarations of the clearest writers, recognise in proselytism a crime civilly imputable.

Whereas, resulting from the preceding facts, it is undeniable that the Madiai labored on many different occasions, and even with success, to make proselytes to the religion newly embraced by them, it only remained to be considered whether in such a fact existed the extremes required by the 60th Art. of the law of 30th November, 1786, for the application of its penal ratification.

Whereas, the extreme of guilty intention in such a crime occurs whenever the intention of the agent is directed to increase the ranks of dissenting sects, to the prejudice of the religion of the state, and that of evil done according to the facts now established in our jurisprudence, it is certified that these acts, though not committed in public places, have been done in the presence of many persons, and are extensively propagated, and engendered a grave scandal.

It is declared evident that impiety was committed by Francesco and Rosa Madiai by means of proselytism to the so-called Evangelical confession, or religion of the pure Gospel, to the prejudice of the Catholic religion, predominant in the Grand Duchy, in the time and way above mentioned.

And whereas the crime of impiety, by means of proselytism, is manifestly contemplated by the 60th article of the law of the country of 30th November, 1786, and is repressed never with less than most exemplary punishment; of which, all the circumstances of the case being considered, it appears that the second degree is proportioned to the delinquency, represented in virtue of successive laws, by the nature and amount of penalty afterwards mentioned.

Whereas the deductions of the defence have all been replied to by the previous proposition of facts and consideration of right.

The following articles having been examined; the 60th of the law of 30th November, 1786; 1, 4, 9, 14 of the Decree of 4th March, 1849, confirmed by the other of 5th May following, and 34 and 35 of the police regulations of 22d November, 1849, and 55 of the above-mentioned law of 30th November, 1786, &c.

Francesco, son of the late Vincenzio Madiai, and Rosa, his wife, are condemned, the former to the punishment of 56 months' seclusion in the prison of forced labor at Volterra, and the latter to 45 months of Ergastolo (the female galleys) calculated in the one case from the 26th of November, 1851, and in the other from the 27th of the same month and year; they are likewise condemned to pay the expenses of the trial, and made subject to the *surveillance* of the Police for three years after the completion of their imprisonment. Such was the termination of this important trial.

OPINIONS OF THE LAWYERS.

The case of the Madiai having been considered and examined by the Signori Salvagnoli, Mori, and Galeotti, three celebrated lawyers of Florence, they having also seen the heads of the defence, gave their full approbation of the ground on which the defence was made, and their conviction of its justice.

The first says:—"The State must be laic not atheistic. And being laic and not atheistic, whether one religion is fixed as its own or not, it can impose none on the citizens, and ought to preserve the public worship or private exercise of every religion. Coming to the case under examination, I cannot but approve of the proofs brought forward by the learned counsel, and I add my firm opinion that no action, recognized as criminal by our laws, can be imputed to the Madiai."

The others add:—"Having examined, with the greatest diligence, the cause of proselytism charged against the Madiai, we are persuaded that not only do these charges, in fact, not exist, but that in this case may be justly claimed the fundamental principles of public right. Therefore, from a sense of truth, and with firm and tranquil conviction, we agree to the line of defence adopted by the learned counsel of the Madiai."

Additional Facts Relating to the Trial.

We give, from authentic Italian sources, the following notices of the trial, which will be read with interest.

The presiding judges (as there was no jury) were Sig. Nervini, who, during the whole trial, appeared very bitter against the culprits; Cocchi, the interrogating Judge, the same who received a hard rebuke during the State trial of Guerrazzi; and Bicchierai, the public prosecutor.

At ten o'clock, A. M., the gendarmes brought three prisoners into the court—Pasquae Casacci, the informer, was the picture of an unhappy man; Francesco Madiai appeared happy to see his wife again, and pressed her hand; and Rosa (his wife) was pale, and trembled with emotion. The few persons present were surprised, and moved with the tranquillity and firmness of the two accused.

At the commencement of the trial, the presiding Judge asked from Francesco Madiai if he was born in the bosom of the Holy Mother, the Roman Catholic Church.

A. Yes, sir, was the reply; but now I am a Christian according to the Gospel.

Q. Who has made you such, and does there exist an act of abjuration amongst those you are united to?

A. My convictions have existed for many years,

but have acquired strength from the study of the word of God.

Q. Who advised you to leave the Catholic faith?

A. Nobody; it has been a matter between God and my own soul.

Q. Have you ever made a public abjuration?

A. Yes, sir.

Q. When and how?

A. When I took the communion in the Swiss church.

Q. Have you distributed among the people any publication contrary to the dogmas of the Roman church?

A. No, sir; the tracts I gave people to read contained only passages of the Holy Scriptures, but nothing of controversy between the two communions.

Q. Did you ever hold religious meetings in your house?

A. Yes, sir.

Q. What did you say and do?

A. That we were all believers in the Evangelical church, and as such we used to congregate and pray.

Here Casacci said to the President that many were Catholics, and Francesco Madiai and Rosa (his wife) persuaded them to leave the Papal church.

Q. What have you to say, Francesco Madiai, against the deposition of the present witness?

A. Those who were yet Catholics desired to become acquainted with the eternal truth, and under such circumstances I could not refuse them admittance to my house.

Q. Have you ever had any religious controversy during the time you spoke against the church?

A. Yes, sir, only when I was provoked; I spoke of the dogmas of the church as contrary to the Bible, but have never used, during this conversation, any disrespectful language.

Hereupon the President ordered Francesco Madiai to sit down. His wife was called to stand up.

Q. Have you changed your religion for any material object?—did you ever receive any pecuniary remuneration?

A. No, sir; I have not changed my former religion lightly, or to please men; in such a case I could have done it when I was in England, where I lived seventeen years.

Q. What, then, could induce you to take that step?

A. The reading of the Bible convinced me of the error and contradictions of the Romish doctrines.

Here the presiding Judge imposed silence on the prisoner.

Q. Have you ever made any public abjuration?

A. Yes, sir; as soon as I became firmly convinced of the truth of the Evangelical doctrine I abandoned the church, and made a public confession of faith by partaking of the Lord's Supper.

Q. Where did the public confession take place?

A. In the Swiss chapel, at Florence, when the former laws of our country gave and protected religious liberty.

Q. Have you, at any time, called the Holy Apostles men of hatred?

A. No, sir; that accusation is totally untrue. I have never been guilty of such a thing, and shall prove the contrary by the words of St. Luke, chapter xxii, from verse 28th to 31st. But the Judge interrupted Rosa Madiai, saying, "We are not speaking about religion now." The defendant replied, "As I am accused of religion, I am to answer and defend myself on that subject."

The President, with a stern look, bid her silence, for the second time.

Q. Have you ever said that the Christian religion has but eight commandments, and that our creed allows fornication?

The prisoner hereupon rose indignantly, and said, in a high tone of voice, that as her only reply to that infamous charge, she should be allowed to say the Ten Commandments, in order that they might judge whether there were eight or ten.

"Silence!" was answered by the court; upon which, being angry, the defendant replied, "that it was not justice to impose silence on one's own defence."

The Judge appeared somewhat milder, and

asked the prisoner if she and her husband observed the ten Commandments?

"Certainly," she answered, "as God dictated them to Moses on Mount Sinai."

Here the word "silence" was repeated, and the examination of Rosa Madiai was closed by the Judge saying "that is sufficient."

The small audience, composed of a few English gentlemen, who had been admitted through the influence of Sir Henry Bulwer, were struck with the simplicity and sincerity of the Madiai.

On the following day the witnesses were examined. On the 6th of June Sig. Maggiorani announced to the court that he was ready for the defence, which he made with so much warmth and feeling as to draw tears even from the eyes of the prosecuting attorney.

Pasquae Casacci, who denied everything, was acquitted of the criminal charge, but was detained to answer two questions against him, by the police, according to the law of April, 1851.

The conduct of the Madiai, during their trial, did them the greatest honor, and awakened the admiration of the audience. They listened to the sentence with great firmness and dignity. Francesco was in perfect peace, and received the final blow in a spirit of holy submission; and the only expression of suffering was squeezing the hand of a friend near by, saying—"There is need of patience—and the comfort, the joy of the Holy Spirit never changes with me, however it may with my poor body. I am always happy. God has been with me all the time of my imprisonment, and He will always be with me as long as I remain in prison, and I am as sure He will be with me unto death."

Conduct of the Prisoners after the Trial.

Rosa Madiai, as soon as she returned to the Bargello prison, knelt and prayed for some time; afterwards she wrote the following letter to her husband:—

"My dear Madiai.—You know that I have always loved you; but how much more ought I to love you now, that we have been together in the battle of the Great King—that we have been beaten, but not vanquished. I hope that, through the merits of Jesus Christ, God our Father will have accepted our testimony, and will give us grace to drink, to the last drop, the portion of that bitter cup which is prepared for us, with returning of thanks. My good Madiai, life is only a day, and a day of grief. Yesterday we were young, to-day we are old. Nevertheless we can say with old Simeon: "Lord, now lettest thou thy servant depart in peace, for mine eyes hath seen thy salvation." Courage, my dear, since we know by the Holy Spirit that this Christ, loaded with opprobrium, trodden down and calumniated, is our Saviour; and we, by his holy light and power, are called to defend the holy cross, and Christ who died for us, receiving his reproaches, that we may afterwards participate in his glory. Do not fear if the punishment be hard. God, who made the chains fall from Peter, and opened the doors of his prison, will never forget us. Keep in good spirits; let us trust entirely in God. Let me see you cheerful, as, I trust, by the same grace you will see me cheerful. I embrace you with my whole heart.

"Your affectionate wife,

"ROSA MADIAI."

Before leaving the Bargello for his final imprisonment, Francesco Madiai applied to be allowed to carry with him a supply of clean linen, clothes, &c. But this was not permitted. He smiled, saying, "Well, all things according to the will of God." He spoke very laudably of his wife, and requested a friend to tell her, "that his prayer was that God would go with them to their prisons, and that he felt sure that God would be their companion there." He was not allowed to see his wife, but was conveyed to his goal of Volterra, and thrown among criminals. A few days after he was removed from the common galleys, and put into cellulary confinement.

The same gentleman who had visited Francesco Madiai while in the city prison, went to see his wife, who, hearing of the sudden departure of her husband, became much oppressed ; and her mind was also tortured by the idea, that, at her advanced age, having always lived amongst virtuous and religious people, she should now be thrown with females of bad conduct. At the same moment, and almost unexpectedly, the prison-keeper brought a message from the police that Rosa Madiai should be taken away from the Bargello and carried to the prisons of Lucca.

At this dreadful notice, in presence of all the attendants and *gendarmes*, she burst into fervent prayer, asking God for more faith, more love to Jesus. Her kind lawyer, Signor Maggiorani, promised to go to Lucca to see that everything that could be permitted should be provided for her: and the physician, who was also present, said that, although it was unusual, he would give a certificate as to the state of her health requiring diet different from that of the common prisoners, as absolutely important to her life.

Having quickly dressed herself, she asked for her bonnet, and to a remark made by one of the jailors, why she did not comb her hair, answered, "For what use, as in a few hours they will cut it off." She bid farewell to all those assistants, and told an English gentleman, in whose service she had been, "Remember me to all the brethren, and tell them, should they be called to follow us, to bear what may be appointed them to suffer, but never to forsake their God." This advice was addressed to the numerous prisoners who were yet under trial in the several prisons of Florence, accused of the same crime for which the Madiai had been condemned.

A special order of the Tuscan government prescribed that the Madiai should be entirely deprived of all religious service and books of their faith, nor should any Protestant clergyman be allowed to visit them—a rule which is not even applied in the same country to the worst criminals. They were soon separated from all the prisoners, and kept in a private and solitary cell—the husband on the hills of Volterra, and the wife at Lucca, a distance of fifty miles. When they are allowed to walk about, it is in a yard, surrounded by walls from which you see nothing but the sky.

Dressed after the manner of all criminals, for the first weeks they were nourished with the common and unhealthy victuals of the prison, and it was but lately that they were allowed to receive victuals from without. In the cell of Rosa Madiai can be seen a large chain hanging to the wall, as a threat in case she should rebel against the prison discipline.

Not long after her arrival at her new prison-house in Lucca, Madame Madiai wrote the following letter to her husband at Volterra:—

"The news I received of your being better, gave me great pleasure, and many were the tears of joy which bathed my cheeks, for two reasons—first, because God has made you worthy of suffering with His beloved Son—second, because He restores your health. Oh, if we knew how to appreciate these humiliations that we suffer, from having acknowledged that there is but one Mediator between God and man! My dear, you say that we expect grace; but allow me to tell you that we have already received that great grace, when, after being separated by force, driven from our dwelling, and our property dispersed as dust before the wind, we have been reduced, you see, to what a state; and yet, with all this, we would not, for all Pharaoh's treasures, as also Moses would not, lose that holy gift which the Holy Ghost has, through His grace, made us, of believing in His divine Word. This, I call a grace, and a very great one. If a star is to shine, it will be the star of justice. We have done no harm to any one; on the contrary, we were injured, having been sold for a few dollars. Our accusers are descendants from Judas. I fear for their souls. I pray that God grant them the tears of Peter, not the punishment of Judas, and that they may one day enjoy the eternal happiness which has been purchased. Were they to come and ask alms from me, I would give it to them as I did formerly, and may God help us! Amen. My dear, let us be ready to do the Father's will, as His Son, our Master, did it. Let us not torment ourselves. Peter trembled while walking on the sea, fearing the flowing of the waters, and forgot that if the Saviour walked towards him, on the same waters, he was not to fear; he feared and cried out—'Lord, save me!' The beneficent hand helped him, saying, 'Man of little faith, why fearest thou?' If the waves of this earth cause us to fear, more shame for us; let us remember the sacred words: 'Although I were to walk in the valley of the shadow of death, I would fear no evil, for Thou art with me.' My dear, rest in the Lord for welfare as well as for sufferings. Every thing passes away. Eternity is the most essential part. Be cheerful, and try to recover. God bless you, and cover you under the shade of His wings, for the grace of our Lord Jesus Christ.

"Your affectionate wife,

"ROSA MADIAI."

The Effect of the Trial and Condemnation upon the Christian Public.

The news that the Madiai had been condemned for having become Protestants, and for proselytism against the Papal Church, (for it amounted to that,) awoke the indignation of all Protestant countries, and even of liberal Roman Catholics, as may be seen from an elaborate article which appeared in the *Journal des Débats* of Paris. At a meeting of the Swiss Evangelical Alliance, held in Geneva, Professor Gaupen was deputed to write to the Earl of Shaftesbury, as President of the "Protestant Alliance" in England, and request the British Christians to take up the case. This led to the holding of public meetings of sympathy in London and other principal cities on the British Isles. Similar meetings were held on the Continent. The Earls of Roden and Cavan, and Captain Trotter, were appointed members of a Deputation to the Grand Duke of Tuscany, to intercede in behalf of these persecuted people. Deputies were also appointed on the Continent, and in the latter part of October, 1852, these gentlemen were on their way to Florence. The Deputation was as follows:—

From England.—The Earl of Roden, Peer of England; Lord Cavan, Peer of Ireland; and Captain Trotter.

France.—Count Agenor de Gasparin, Deputy of France under Louis Philippe; and M. De Mimont, ex-Captain of Etat the Major.

Germany.—Count de Bonin, Captain of the Royal Guards of his Majesty the King of Prussia; and Count Albert de Pourtalès, former Minister at Constantinople.

Holland.—Mr. Elout de Soetherwoude, Chancellor of the Royal Court of Amsterdam.

Switzerland.—Colonel Tronchin and Count de Saint George.

Upon the arrival of these distinguished men at the Tuscan capital, the following correspondence took place.

"FLORENCE, Oct. 24, 1852.

To His Excellency the Duke of Casigliano,
Secretary of Foreign Affairs of Tuscany.

"SIR—We apply to your Excellency in order that you may beg of his Imperial Highness to grant us an audience. We wish to have the honor of placing before him the expressions of sympathy that Mr. and Mrs. Madiai have obtained in every Protestant community. We come as simple delegates of Evangelical Christians of several countries. We acknowledge that as such, we have no right to implore the favor of a reception from his Imperial Highness; we consider it as an important point that a religious attempt be not misunderstood for an intervention, or, as we would term it, a political expression. For this purpose we come without the mediation of any ministers accredited to the government of the Grand Duchy, hoping that our demand will meet with a welcome acceptance, being only in our own name.

"His Imperial Highness will, no doubt, appreciate the sentiment which such demeanor inspires us with, as well as that which induces us to recommend, most respectfully, to his consideration, Mr. and Mrs. Madiai.

"Receive, Duke, the assurance of our most profound esteem, RODEN, A. DE GASPARIN,
CAVAN, F. DE MINONT,
TROTTER."

Answer of the Minister.

"FLORENCE, October 25, 1852.

"MY LORD,—I have placed before my sovereign the letter addressed to me on the 24th inst. by several distinguished persons, among whom appears your name. His Imperial and Royal Highness appreciates your form of request, as he certainly would have deprecated any political expression, and the honorable diplomatic agents residing near this court would doubtless have reprobated such a course.

"The two mentioned Madiai, husband and wife, Tuscan subjects, have been condemned by the ordinary tribunals to five years imprisonment, for the crime of Protestant propaganda, which is punished by our laws, as it attacks the religion of the State. The punishment inflicted on them is merely the application of those same laws, and their appeal has been rejected.

"His Imperial and Royal Highness, reserving to himself the power of exercising his high privilege in the manner he considers most convenient, could not allow the intervention of any one whatsoever in an affair which concerns the administration of justice in our States, and his manner of proceeding towards his own subjects. My royal sovereign, aware of the benevolent sentiments with which you are inspired in taking this step, but not considering that he must allow an intervention of any kind in this transaction, directs me to inform you, my lord, that he is sorry not to be able to grant the audience implored by yourself and the others who have signed the letter addressed to me.

"Receive, my lord, and communicate to those gentlemen, the assurance of my very profound esteem. THE DUKE OF CASSIGLIANO."

"To the right Honorable, the Earl of Roden,
Peer of England, at Florence."

As soon as the deputation, who were in permanent sitting, had received this answer, they agreed to write an address to the Grand Duke, and sent it, as is customary, enclosed in the following letter to the Minister of Foreign Affairs:—

"To His Excellency the Duke of Casigliano,
Secretary of Foreign Affairs of Tuscany,"

SIR,—"We have received the letter by which your Excellency does us the honor of informing us that His Imperial Highness has appreciated the form given to our request, and does not, however, think of granting us the implored audience, but reserves to himself the use of his high privilege in the way which he will consider most convenient.

"All that remains for us to do now is to perform our mission as well as we can, by conveying to your Excellency the expressions of those sentiments which we had been charged with presenting to His Imperial Highness, and had placed in the enclosed address.

"We hope that if His Imperial Highness will vouchsafe to read them, he will perceive nothing but what is becoming to the religious character of our peaceful intervention, and the profound respect that abides within us.

"Please, accept Duke, this new testimony of our very profound esteem.

RODEN, A. DE GASPARIN,
CAVAN, A. DE BONIN,
TROTTER, DE MIMONT."

"P. S.—In order not to make your excellency wait for the answer which is due to you by us, we sign this letter before the arrival of the other deputies, who are already on their way to Florence, and whom we consider as here present, aware of our demand. They are Albert de Pourtalès, from Berlin; Colonel Tronchin; the Count of St. George, from Geneva; and the Counsellor Elout de Soetherwoude, from Amsterdam."

ADDRESS.

"IMPERIAL AND ROYAL HIGHNESS.—Your Imperial and Royal Highness knows with what views we have the honor of appearing before you. We not only abstained from having recourse to a diplomatic intervention, which would have compromised the exclusively religious character of our mission, but we openly show, from this very moment, the wish that this mission may never henceforth serve as a pretext to any political action.

"We are but simple Christians, and representatives of millions of other Christians, who use no other arms than prayer, no other strength than that of their Divine Master. Our embassy is quite of a new kind, and we believe is to be considered as a testimonial of respect which is shown to the Prince to whom it is addressed.

"Our brethren have said to us:—Go, not in the name of this or of that Protestant power, but in the name of the Lord Jesus; go and acquaint the sovereign of Tuscany with the expression of profound sympathy excited by the condition of Mr. and Mrs. Madiai; we hope that such general sympathy will be taken into consideration by your Imperial and Royal Highness.

"We will not attempt, your Highness, to judge about the convenience of the law, nor its application. It is certainly not our business to meddle with the legislation or administration of justice in your States. We only feel the want of adding a word of justification to our steps, which is, that we never refuse to those contrary to our faith, what we wish in favor of our Protestant brethren. The Roman Catholic is free in the countries which we represent. Your Imperial and Royal Highness understands the meaning of these words. How could we ever have dared to address you this petition in favor of our brethren, the Madiai, if we knew not how to accept the condition of granting freedom to Roman Catholics? We should have omitted the profound respect due to your Imperial and Royal Highness had we hesitated in speaking thus.

"Respect is not only on our lips, but we feel it in us. The Evangelical Christians who have sent us hither, have all learned, from a study of holy books to respect constituted powers, and their prayers for your Imperial and Royal Highness have joined to those which are now offered in all parts of Europe and America for our brethren Madiai.

"We sincerely hope, your Highness, that your answer will be such as to afford full consolation to those who sent us.

"Roden, Gasparan,
A. de Bonin, Cavan,
De Mamont, Trotter."

Thus terminated the efforts of the Deputation, so far as the Tuscan Government was concerned. Soon afterwards they left Florence for their respective countries, to make report to those who had sent them. It would seem that they left Italy with the hope that the prisoners would, after a few weeks or months, be released, through the grace of the Grand Duke—a hope which has been utterly disappointed.

Correspondence between the Deputation and the Converts in Tuscany.

Before the Deputation left Florence they received the following interesting letter from a committee (whose names must remain unknown to the world) of the Converts from Popery in that city and its vicinity, and made a suitable reply:—

"To the Christian Brethren forming the various Deputations sent to appeal in favor of Francesco and Rosa Madiai, held Prisoners in Tuscany for the cause of the Gospel.

"*Beloved brethren in the Lord*,—The evangelical Christians in Tuscany, greatly moved by the earnest proof of Christian love shown to them by many brethren of various countries and languages, but united to them in one common bond of faith, desire to express their thankfulness and gratitude for the love that has led you, unsolicited by them, to come hither for the sole purpose of endeavoring to alleviate the sufferings of our brother and sister, Francesco and Rosa Madiai, now enduring hard bondage for reading the Word of Life, and for the open and free confession of that truth, believed and held by them with that constancy and steadfastness alone worthy of those who, like faithful sheep, know the voice of the 'true Shepherd' that died to save them, and 'follow him whithersoever He goeth;' but for which steadfastness they are now accused of impiety.

"We believe it unnecessary to recapitulate the painful history of their long and severe sufferings, inasmuch as you are already well-informed of all that has happened to us, and have with so much love watched all the trials we have been subject to within the last few years. You have heard, that having been bred up and instructed to assume at least the outward garb of religion, even if accompanied by a fatal and passive indifference, provided we did not openly question the customs and traditions imposed upon us; many of us became either solely wrapped up in the political vicissitudes of our unhappy country, or, 'ignorant of *God's* righteousness,' went about 'to establish our own righteousness, not submitting ourselves unto the righteousness of God.' Romans, x. 3. In this fatal delusion we must have remained, had we not had free access to the unadulterated Word of God, 'able to make us wise unto salvation.' It is through His mercy and grace alone that we now abide faithful unto that Word, notwithstanding the many trials daily renewed against us by our rulers. For these, indeed, we continually pray, knowing the many difficulties and obstacles they have to contend with from those who are the worst enemies to the diffusion of God's

Word, and whose influence our rulers have sought to enlist, by concessions in their favor, and by severity against those who have separated themselves, under the idea that to uphold the predominant religion of the State is the best guarantee for the peace and prosperity of the country.

"We are truly sorry that at this time, especially, we cannot personally render you an open testimony of our gratitude and love for the singular proof you have given us of your sympathy with our suffering brethren; but you are well aware that we are not permitted now even to meet together for mutual edification, and that we are obliged to abstain from assembling ourselves together, even for the sole purpose of worshipping God, through fear of either imprisonment or exile, and the consequent distress of our families. We are thus in difficulty between the laws of our country and the express laws of our God. Heb. x. 25. We would gladly forego many of the rights of citizens, or willingly bear any other burthen, if in exchange we could meet in the name of our Lord.

"But though we cannot openly and collectively offer you the expression of our gratitude for the sympathy which you have so manifested towards us in our trials and sufferings, we cannot be hindered from offering up our prayers to the 'Father of Mercies' and 'God of all Grace,' that He may crown your mission with success, and may grant us better days, when we may 'worship God in quietness, none daring to make us afraid.'

"If, however, it must needs be that we should yet suffer for the truth, we commit ourselves in confidence to our Father in Heaven, who will not permit us to be tried above what we are able to bear, and who has graciously assured His people that 'as their days are, so shall their strength be.' Deut. xxxiii. 25. And we abide the issue of these trials with the calm assurance that He who permits them, will overrule them for His own glory, and for our good; and that the things that befall us shall turn out, as in the early days of His Church, rather to the furtherance of the Gospel.

"One other matter we cannot pass by. We have been accused of making a profession of the Gospel for the sole purpose of endeavoring to undermine the present political state of the country; but your deputation, coming from so many friendly States, is a clear and undeniable proof that we have not been actuated by political motives in searching, as we have done, the Scriptures of truth.

"We entreat you, that when you return again to your native lands you will convey to our brethren who sent you the expression of our deepest gratitude; and tell them that we feel encouraged and sustained by their sympathy, and that the moral support of all the evangelical Christians of Europe is of the greatest value and consequence to God's people in this land, who desire to know for themselves the Word of Eternal Life. Above all things, request them to unite their prayers with ours, that the Lord may uphold us in all our need, and prepare us for all that He has prepared for us; and that His Word may have free course in this land and be glorified. Finally, that in all that concerns us, His will, and not ours, may be done. Our trust is in Him from whom our strength cometh, and whose grace is sufficient for us; and for the joy set before us we gladly endure the passing afflictions of the present time, knowing that 'He who hath loved us and washed us from our sins in His own blood' shall guide us at last 'to the rest that remaineth,' when 'the Lamb which is in the midst of the throne shall feed us, and shall lead us to the living fountains of water, and God shall wipe away all tears from our eyes.'

"May our Lord and Saviour Jesus Christ, who hath abolished death, and hath brought life and immortality to light through the Gospel, strengthen, comfort, and bless you above all that you can ask or think; and to His name be all the praise."

"Florence, October 29th, 1852."

Reply of the Deputation to the Address of the Evangelical Christians in Tuscany.

"*Beloved Brethren in the Lord Jesus Christ.*—Though we entertained no doubt of the warm sympathy you would feel for us while exerting ourselves in favor of a suffering brother and sister of your own body, yet we must assure you of the joy that has filled our hearts at the address we have just received. This joy is increased, not only by the Christian character of the sentiments therein contained, but by our knowledge that it emanates from a body *so numerous* that it makes us lift up our hearts to the Lord with thankfulness for the fact, that even in this land, where darkness so long prevailed, He has been adding daily to the church those that should be saved. Acts, ii. 47.

"As our own mission has been throughout free of every worldly or political object, we have the less scruple in exhorting you to continue in the same course. We know that the more truly you are evangelical Christians, the better subjects you will be; mindful of that Scriptnre, that, 'Whosoever resisteth the power resisteth the ordinance of God.' Rom. xiii. 2. 'Let not then your good be evil spoken of.' Rom. xiv. 16. This counsel we would tender to you, in all simplicity; ever mindful, however, of that last appeal to be made to all rulers in extreme cases. 'Whether it be right in the sight of God to hearken unto you, more than unto God, judge ye' Acts, xiv. 10. followed as it must be, in manners of conscience, by the reply. 'We ought to obey God rather than men.' Acts, v. 29.

It is unnecessary to suggest to you that we must

all be prepared with patience to endure suffering for conscience sake. For *us*, to hear of your sufferings is grievous; for *you*, it is even 'thankworthy; if a man for conscience sake towards God, endure grief, suffering wrongfully,' 1 Pet. ii. 19. for (most glorious of consequences!) 'if, when ye do well and suffer for it, ye take it patiently, this is acceptable with God.' 1 Pet. ii. 20. The remedy is in God's hand. He has already filled the hearts of those who have not been 'counted worthy to suffer,' with sympathy for those who have; and if ye only pursue your present course of submission to His will, and to those appointed under Him—of love for the truth, strengthened rather than weakened by persecution; and of close union, as brethren and fellow-sufferers for Christ's sake—ye must not doubt of that help from the Lord, who has promised to listen to the prayers of them that ask Him.

"We know that if a man's ways please the Lord, 'He maketh even his enemies to be at peace with him.' Prov. xvi. 7.

"Already the prayers of hundreds of thousands of Protestant Christians are raised to Him, not only in favor of the Madiai, whose sufferings are known, but for the unknown multitude who, like you, are hindered in their course by those who love not the light.

"That these acts will strengthen and not weaken your faith, we are confirmed in believing; while we witness in your ardor of love for the Saviour, little dreamed of by many who have free liberty to confess Him, and to call upon Him, to feast on His words of comfort, and to join in the pure worship of Him as the sole Mediator between God and man. Thus, then, must we continue, in hope, in faith, in love, to offer up this prayer for you—'The God of all grace, who has called us unto His eternal glory by Christ Jesus, after that ye have suffered awhile, make you perfect, stablish, strengthen, settle you.'" 1 Pet. v. 10.

Lord Roden's Visit to the imprisoned Madiai.

Before leaving Tuscany, the Earl of Roden requested permission of the Tuscan Government to visit the Madiai in their prisons. The following are the "notes" which he made of those visits. They cannot be read by any Christian without deep emotion.

Note of my Conversation with Francesco Madiai in the prison at Volterra, 3rd November, 1852.

"Having arrived here last night, I proceeded at ten o'clock this morning to the great prison, allotted to persons convicted of the worst crimes; containing within its walls at the present time above 500 criminals. This most imposing building is situated on the summit of the heights of Volterra, 1,800 feet above the level of the sea. I waited on the direttore, who received me with civility. I presented to him my passport, that he might identify me as the person whom he had received orders from the Government to admit to visit the prisoner, Francesco Madiai. He introduced me to the sub-direttore, desiring him to conduct me to Madiai's room. We passed through a very long corridor, with cells on either side, and reached the door of the infirmary, where Francesco was confined. I was shown into a small room, where the window was on a level with the table, and there was air and light in abundance. Francesco rose from his chair when the sub-direttore told him who I was; he then shut the door and retired, so that I had full opportunity to converse with the prisoner alone. In about a quarter of an hour the sub-direttore returned with the doctor. I thanked them both for their kindness to Francesco, particularly the latter; and I told Madiai, in their hearing, that I was at the head of a deputation which had come from England, France, Germany, Switzerland and Holland, to implore the Grand Duke's clemency towards him and his wife; that, in so doing, we were not only influenced by compassion for them, and the deepest sympathy for their sufferings, but that our special object was to endorse the principle which they had maintained, and for which they were now suffering, namely, that every individual in the world had a right to read the Word of God without note or comment; and that that principle was near and dear to our hearts as Christians. Neither the sub-direttore nor the doctor made any remark to this; but the latter said, that Francesco's health had improved, that all fever had left him, though there was still much weakness. I then told Francesco that I had visited him and his wife at the request of my brother deputies, who, together with all who loved and valued the Word of God, were warmly attached to them both, and were thankful to God for the confession which they had been enabled to make, and for the support which He had given them under their heavy trials, during fifteen months' incarceration, several months of which I was aware had been spent in the *Bargello*, the common prison of Florence, where the treatment of them had been most cruel—indeed, barbarous.

"The sub-direttore and doctor having retired, he spoke much to me of the state of his health, saying he was better; but in his weak and reduced frame I could too plainly see the effects of all through which he had passed, and, although comparatively better, I have no doubt that a much longer confinement must terminate in his death. He talked of the comfort which he had in the Scriptures; he found the testimony of the Lord Jesus in them his great support; he cared little for other books in comparison with the Word of God; he was allowed the Roman Catholic Bible by Martini, with notes.

"I told him that his wife, whom I had seen two days before, requested me to tell him that she was well. He was looking forward with great hope to his speedy liberation, and seemed much disappointed at the failure of our application. I said that the King of Prussia had taken a special interest in their case, and had sent a nobleman from Berlin, Count Arnim, to plead their cause before the Grand Duke. His eyes then filled with tears, and he exclaimed, 'How can I ever be grateful enough to God for His mercies to me!' He spoke of his own nothingness, and that therefore it could only have been God who had put it into the hearts of kings and nobles, and of Christians of distant countries, to be so interested in their behalf. He added, that he felt that he was in God's hands, and that he would do with him as He pleased.

"I found in Francesco Madiai a simple-minded Christian, greatly depressed and worn down by severe suffering, mental and bodily. He made no complaints, and spoke with the greatest respect of the Grand Duke, his sovereign, to whom, I had previously heard, he had been always a most attached and loyal subject. He evidently would have entered more at length into the particulars of his case, but I told him that I already knew them. When I asked him if I could do anything for him, he said, 'Nothing but to pray for him.' I then offered up a short prayer with him for the continuance of God's favor and support towards him and his wife, and bade him farewell with feelings kindred to those with which I had taken leave of his poor wife."

"RODEN."

We subjoin to the Earl of Roden's "Notes," an extract of a letter from a Christian friend in Florence, dated some weeks after the Deputation had left, to show that the Government of Tuscany has increased the rigor of its course.

"You are aware of the two new decrees, the first of which re-establishes the pain of death for crimes of public violence against the government and against religion; and the second authorizes the police to search and imprison, without judgment or sentence from the ordinary tribunals. These decrees were published on the 17th November, and on the 18th, at five o'clock A. M. Angiolo Guarducci was arrested, he being still in bed, his lodgings searched, and himself taken to the Murate, where he has been for the last fortnight.

"We have passed many a happy hour during the presence in our city of so many dear brethren from several cities; but the sun which shone for a short time was soon overclouded. Lord Roden went to see Rosa Madiai on the 31st Oct. and Francesco on the 3d of November. Their faithful and alway devoted friend Mr. C——, saw Francesco on the 6th; but some days after, hearing that he was confined to his bed, and wishing to see him, this consolation was refused him. Recent and severe orders only allowed one visit a month. Sir H. Bulwer's interference, to mitigate this order, was useless. We are aware that since Mr. C—— left, Madiai's physical weakness has been very great. For several days he refused his medicines, and even his coffee and milk, through fear of being poisoned. On Saturday this gentleman returned to Volterra to see the prisoner—the time prefixed since his last visit being expired."

PROCEEDINGS IN AMERICA.

CHAPTER I.

A Notice of a Meeting in Metropolitan Hall. Statement of Facts.—Resolutions adopted.—Declaration of Principles. —Dr. Bethune's Address.—Popish opposition.—Meeting in Newark.—Meeting in Baltimore.—Resolutions of New-York Legislature.—Resolutions off United States Senate.—Mr. Everett's Letter.

Americans had watched the movements of the Papal Powers in Europe, and with grief had seen the recently brightened prospects of the friends of freedom, and of Evangelical Religion there, rapidly receding from them, and Popery with primitive energy, seeking to re-establish itself, to regain and to hold its former dominion, by the most unjustifiable and cruel measures. Fines, imprisonment, banishment, confiscation of goods, and death, were common inflictions on those who did not conform to all its requsitions. The Madiai fell under its displeasure, but they were not alone. There were many cases very similar, which were known to the people of this country; but by the directions of an overruling Providence the Madiai were made to hold a prominent place in the public view.

Previously there had been no little conversation

in social circles in regard to them, and an occasional paragraph in Newspapers concerning them had also appeared. But in the Autumn of 1852 a crisis seemed forming. Large numbers of all classes who had been interested in them, and in their associates in suffering in Tuscany for the cause of Christ, began to talk of some public expression of American Sentiments upon the subject. The feeling of sympathy for the sufferers grew daily in intensity; and in the month of December the public mind was ripe for the expression of its deep and sacred emotions, its utter abhorrence of intolerance and persecution on account of religious faith and practice.

At the suggestion of a joint committee from the American and Foreign Christian Union, and The Evangelical Alliance, who were appointed to make arrangements for a public meeting of the "friends of religious liberty," without regard to sect or party, the following call, signed by thirty men of the first respectability in the city of New-York, was published in several of the leading Secular and Religious Newspapers, viz.

"The undersigned would respectfully suggest the propriety of convening a public meeting, to be held at Metropolitan Hall on Friday evening, January 7th, for the purpose of expressing the sympathy of the Christian community, and of the friends of religious liberty, with the 'Madiai' family and others, imprisoned in the Grand Duchy of Tuscany for possessing and reading the Holy Scriptures, and to consider what measures may properly be taken for the relief of their present sufferings, and for their release from imprisonment."

In accordance with this Call, on Friday evening January 7th, 1853, an immense concourse of people assembled at the Metropolitan Hall. The Honorable Jacob A. Westervelt, the Mayor of the city, presided, and was supported by a large number of Vice-Presidents, lay and clerical.

The meeting having been organized, by reading the "Call," and the choice of its officers, was opened with prayer by the Rev. Thomas De Witt, D. D. The Rev. Robert Baird, D. D. then submitted a brief statement, comprising the leading political events in Tuscany during a few past years—the religious condition of the people—facts concerning the Madiai,—their social relations, conversion to christianity, quiet and exemplary lives, arrest, trial, condemnation and imprisonment,—and the efforts which had been made in Europe, but in vain, for their release.

In behalf of the committee of arrangements for the meeting, the Rev. W. Patton, D. D. then submitted the following resolutions, which were received by the audience with great favor, viz.

RESOLUTIONS.

"Whereas this meeting has learned, with profound sorrow, that Sig. Madiai and his wife, together with other worthy persons in the Grand Duchy of Tuscany, have been torn from their homes and thrown into prison, subject to coercive discipline, or otherwise persecuted, for possessing and reading the Bible; and whereas it is believed that general manifestations of public opinion have been found in all civilized countries to exert a happy influence upon governments as well as upon those who suffer:

"*Resolved*, 1. That this meeting would express its deep sympathy for these sufferers for conscience sake in their severe trials, and offer its prayers to Heaven that they may be sustained by God's grace under them, and that these persecutions may have a speedy termination.

"*Resolved*, 2. That his Excellency, the President of the United States be, and hereby is, requested to exert his kindly influence in such manner as he may deem most judicious and most compatible with the duties of his official position, in behalf of these people, in the hope that the Government of Tuscany, in compliance with a respectful expression of the personal wishes of the Chief Magistrate of a nation which welcomes all who come to its shores, whatever may be their creed, and gives them equal and complete religious liberty, may at least allow Signor Madiai and his wife to quit their prisons, and emigrate, if so disposed, to our country, at our expense.

"*Resolved*, 3. That this great meeting, convened without distinction of sect or party, and composed of friends of Religious Liberty, avails itself of the occasion, in this solemn and formal manner, to declare to Europe and to the whole world, that an experience, running through many years, has demonstrated to our unanimous judgment the safety, harmony and prosperity which entire religious liberty secures both to the State and to Religion.

"*Resolved*, 4. That this meeting firmly believes that it is the duty of the Government of the United States to protect all our citizens in their religious rights whilst residing or sojourning in foreign lands; approves in the fullest manner of a noble attempt of a distinguished Senator from Michigan, (Gen. Cass,) to call the attention of the Government and the public to this important subject; and entertains the confident hope that this Government will speedily secure to its citizens, by the express stipulations of international treaties, the right to worship God according to the dictates of their conscience in every foreign land.

"*Resolved*, 5. That this meeting is of the opinion that the benevolence which the Gospel teaches and inspires, should lead the Government of these United States, and the Governments of other countries which enjoy the blessings of religious liberty, and have experienced its advantages, to exert a judicious, proper, and peaceful influence to secure these blessings and advantages to all nations which do not possess them.

"*Resolved*, 6. Finally, that whereas the Bible is acknowledged by all Christians to be from God, and to contain a revelation of His will concerning men, and lies at the foundation of Christianity, this meeting affirms, in the most emphatic manner, its unwavering conviction, that as every man is responsible to God alone for his religious belief, that no government, civil or ecclesiastical, has the *right* to forbid any man to possess and read that sacred volume for himself, or read it to his family, to his neighbors, to his friends, and to all who desire to hear it.

"*Additional Resolution.* That inasmuch as we have learned that several of these persecuted people are in exile and in want, and others in prison, and that their families are reduced to great distress, and some of them to utter destitution, this meeting recommends that contributions be made by the benevolent, without delay, for their relief, and that a committee be appointed to receive and expend the funds which may be raised."

The Rev. John Kenneday, D. D. of Brooklyn, N. Y.—the Rev. N. Murray, D. D. of Elizabethtown, N. J. and the Rev. William Hague, D. D. of Newark, N. J. respectively, and in the order named, delivered very able and interesting addresses, which were received by the meeting with very great satisfaction, and warm expressions of applause.

The Congregation then rose, and sung, standing,

to the tune of Old Hundred, the 117th Psalm, beginning "From all who dwell below the skies," when at its close the Rev. E. R. Fairchild, D. D. in behalf of the Committee, read the following Declaration, which was also received with approbation, viz:

DECLARATION.

"1. It has been proposed to invoke the influence of the President of the United States to induce the government of Tuscany to pursue a milder policy, because it is believed that the affair of the Madiai has reached such a point, that, in answer to a kind request coming from the Chief Magistrate of this country, not in the way of ordinary diplomacy, or as a political question, but as an act of personal favor to him, and as a favor to this nation, clemency may be shown to these sufferers, and they may be allowed to come to us. This request is made the more readily to our worthy Chief Magistrate, because it is within our knowledge that a similar influence has been not once but several times exerted in favor of clemency by several of his predecessors, and not in vain. This happened in relation to a persecution, a few years ago, at Hamburg, the massacre of the Jews at Damascus, as well as in other instances.

"2. With equal readiness should we unite with our fellow-citizens in invoking that influence in the case of any persons suffering for conscience' sake, whoever they might be, whenever it can be shown that such interposition, personal rather than official, would be likely to prove effectual.

"3. Whilst this meeting, fully believing that God has given to no man the right to hold error, or practice a false worship, yet that, in this respect he is accountable to Him who alone is Lord of the conscience, who has given him His word to enlighten and guide him, if he will submit to its teachings; and that no man, no combination of men, nor human government, has the right to compel men to believe as *they* do, "under pains and penalties;" therefore this meeting reprobates that state of things, in any country, by which dissent from the Established Church is viewed and treated as constructive treason.

"4. It is not the object of this meeting to boast of our political institutions, or to meddle with questions of a political nature. We have no desire to wound the feelings of other nations by touching questions that relate to the forms of the civil government—questions which we hold, that every nation has the exclusive right to decide for itself, and may justly demand that its decisions shall be respected.

"5. Neither have we come together to abuse the rulers of any country in Europe, or of any other part of the world; but, appreciating in some good degree the difficulties under which some of them and their governments lie at present, we would set before them what we have found to be so beneficial to all concerned in our country, and make some suggestions which may (with God's blessing) not be without use to them.

"6. This meeting would consider the subject before them, not as a Protestant or Roman Catholic question, but as one which concerns the interests of humanity entire, especially the interests and honor of Christendom. We desire liberty of conscience for all, whoever they may be, and we reprobate and stigmatise persecution on religious grounds, wherever it may exist. We live under a government, we are happy to say, whose constitutional provisions guarantee to the population (native and foreign) the enjoyment of the rights of conscience, the rights of private and public worship, the right to hold and to propagate their religious opinions respecting doctrines and worship in all proper and peaceable ways—a government which has made no law, that we are aware of, with the intention of preventing men from holding or imparting to their fellow-men such opinions as may seem to them right on the subject of religion.

"7. The religious liberty so fully enjoyed by all in the United States justifies us in appealing to the liberality of the rulers and governments of Europe, to concede all the liberty of worship and of opinion which may be consistent with internal peace, and due to national comity. The people of the United

States, chiefly Protestants, cannot look upon the punishment of men for no other offence than Protestantism, without that dissatisfaction which must strongly act upon all Protestant people, and prepare a state of opinion which may one day be very unfavorable to the peace of the world.

"8. Still further: the people of the United States, when conflagration or famine overwhelms with distress or ruin any other people, do not stop to inquire into the religious or political opinions of the sufferers, but fly promptly to their relief, as has been twice done in relation to Madeira, and also to Ireland, Scotland, and Greece. This liberality on our part entitles us to, at least, a respectful hearing, when we speak of religious liberty to the nations of the earth, especially as we have had ample experience of its blessed influence.

"9. Christendom has long submitted to a *law of nations.* And even *the comity of nations*, if it has not commanded so general an assent, has at least exerted a wide and perceptible influence. But a *public opinion of nations* is rapidly growing into power, and its influence will be far more effectual and controling than either. The facilities of travelling, the wonders of the telegraph, the increase of knowledge, are opening the way for an interchange of opinions which must remove many difficulties, and thus bring about a unity of sentiment on very many subjects on which men have heretofore been divided. It will become a matter of necessity that rulers and governments prepare for this change, and so modify their laws and regulations as to make due concessions to this new state of things."

The Rev. George W. Bethune, D. D. of Brooklyn, New-York, next addressed the meeting in a very able and appropriate speech, and which was received with very great enthusiasm. That the reader may enter into the spirit, the feelings, and the high and worthy aims of the meeting, the following, but greatly condensed report of this excellent speech, which occupied nearly an hour in its delivery, is submitted:—

DR. BETHUNE'S ADDRESS.

'The Rev. Dr. Bethune said this was to him a most solemn occasion. He felt as if he were called again into the presence of centuries long past. He seemed to hear those sublime words ringing in his ears: 'I believe in the Holy Ghost, and in the holy Catholic church, and in the communion of saints.' There is but one head, and but one body; and wherever there is one who believes in Jesus Christ, there is a member of that church; and if one member suffers, all the members suffer with it. If we have the Holy Ghost within us, if we have become vitally united to the body of our blessed Lord by a living faith, there is not one of us whose heart is not bleeding with those beloved Christians who are now crushed beneath the foot of the oppressor; and we must, before God, who gave us hearts and faith, speak out. I am sure we must all feel it, and our sympathies must find relief; and if it reach no further than to give us relief from this pent-up emotion, this meeting is a blessing to the freemen and inhabitants of New-York. (Applause.) I said I felt as if I were called into centuries long past away. We read of the sufferings of the primitive Christians —we read of them who were stoned and sawn asunder—who sang amidst the smoke of their fires —who perished in dungeons with the long pain of fatal hunger; and, until a very short time ago, we had felt, as Christians, that these days were past. There were some prophecies that, interpreted in a particular light, seemed to tell us that the days of that persecution might return, but we had been long in the habit of feeling that those days had gone.

"It is not long since we had the privilege to welcome the stranger among us, and it was a higher privilege to wolcome those exiles from the island of Madeira. Then, for the first time, we were permitted to see the 'confessors,' such as are now canonized by that same Church of Rome. And now we are told that two obscure individuals, in the midst of that church, are incarcerated and treated as felons, for no crime but reading the Bible. From my heart I sympathise with those two persons, that brother and sister in Christ; but much remains yet behind to be filled up of the sufferings of Christ. There remains yet a necessity for the sufferings of the people of God, to prove in the first place the evil of that spirit which exalts itself against the Scriptures; and, in the second place, to prove the divinity of that faith which upholds the soul above torture and imprisonment and death.

"This proves that the spirit of that power is unchanged. It is impossible for an American, brought up from his childhood amidst the light and liberty, and privileges which we enjoy in this land—it is impossible for him to conceive the tyranny and oppression which exist in the Old World, and when we tell him of it, he tells us that we are calumniating our brethren, and that it is not right to bring such charges against men because their ancestors in past centuries have been guilty of crimes, and that the growing light of science and the interchange of philanthropic feeling have wrought a great revolution in the spirit of that church which was formerly recognized as a church of persecution. Here is a fact rising up before us, which tells us that the spirit which persecuted the Albigenses is still there, not dead, but rampant and ready, so far as it has the power, to crush now, as it was ready to crush five hundred years ago. Am I wrong in this? I see a brother here upon the stage who told me once, in preaching preparatory to the sacrament, he took occasion to explain the fallacy of the doctrine of transubstantiation held by the Catholic Church, and that one of his parishioners complained of his slandering the Catholics; "for we all know," said the man, "that nobody can believe such nonsense." This was the light he took of it, and precisely in the same manner do we find people believing it impossible that the spirit of persecution can still exist as it existed in former years. The spirit of Antichrist is the same at all times. The spirit of Christ says, "Search the Scriptures," and wherever there comes a spirit which forbids you to search the Scriptures, you may depend upon it that there is the spirit of Antichrist, because it is opposed to it. (Applause.) And now we know that this oppression exists, does it not become us to aid the oppressed? Are we not a republic? and are we not the only nation on the face of the earth—except it be the little republic on the shores of Liberia—in which religious liberty is entire. (Applause.) Since we are in this country as republicans, and bearing our testimony to the value of republican principles in the face of the whole earth, should we not believe that it is part of our mission not only to enjoy what God has sent us, but to diffuse it to others? This is the only country in which the principle of religious liberty has been permitted to work itself out; and as all our churches have flourished and grown strong, and been a blessing to us under the system, I say it is our duty, not as Protestants merely, but as freemen, to lift up our voice against religious oppression wherever it may exist. (Loud applause.) Now I wish to speak a few words in relation to the Romish Church. What is the meaning of the words "Protestant country," as applied to the United States? I now read as follows:—

I suppose that at last it will come down to signify nothing more than that the majority of the inhabitants are Protestants; but has it never occurred to those who would make such an objection, that majorities and minorities are mere accidents, liable to change! whereas the constitution is a principle and not an accident; "its great"—and mark you this—"its great and unappreciable value is that it prescribes the duties of the majority, and protects with equal and impartial justice the rights of the manority. In this country the constitution of the United States says the majority shall rule."

God grant it! "Now, in pursuance of the constitution, this is neither a Protestant nor a Catholic country, but a broad land of civil and religious freedom and equality to all." This is the eulogium pronounced upon the constitution of the United States by Archbishop Hughes. Now, I have not the honor of knowing that gentleman personally, but we are sufficiently well known to the public to warrant my not waiting for an introduction, and I call upon him in the name of the liberties which his Church has enjoyed—in the name of that freedom which every Protestant in this house, that is worthy the name of Protestant, is willing to accord to every Roman Catholic in the land—I call upon him in gratitude to the Baltimores and Williamses, and those whose spirits made that constitution of ours free from every stain of religious restraint—I call upon him to join us in calling upon the Duke of Tuscany to set free these people. (Tremendous applause.) If this oppression be not the work of Roman Catholicism, he cannot, he will not refuse to join in the extension of that principle over which he rejoices. (Cheers.) If he does not join us we shall believe that such oppression is part and parcel of Roman Catholicism, and that if they had the power here, they would act like the Duke of Tuscany. This is the point to which we come. We have stronger sympathies in one cause than another, and it is possible that I may have them; but I verily believe, if I know my own heart, that if this were a case of religious oppression of a Jew or Turk, much more the oppression of a Roman Catholic, who yet I hold to be a fellow Christian—I may say my indignation would be as strong as it is now; and I would lift up my feeble voice in advocacy of the great principle, that, let man be Jew, Turk, Papist or Protestant, let him alone. (Loud applause.) Let him talk with his God, and let his God talk with him; and therefore it is not as a Protestant, but as a Christian citizen of a free land, that I am glad to see my Catholic fellow-citizens as free as myself—therefore it is that I desire to protest against this oppression, and I call upon my Catholic brethren to join with me in the protest. (Applause.) It will not come; depend upon it, it will not.

Every one who knows anything about Italy for years since, is aware that this very Duke of Tuscany was so kind, so clement, and so lenient a prince, that he may be said to have been the best beloved of all European sovereigns, unless it may be perhaps the Emperor of Russia, who is regarded with a sort of religious affection; and I will tell you more, that if that conspiracy which broke out some years ago to consolidate Italy into one kingdom had been successful, the leaders would have placed him at the head of the kingdom. And why? Because of his liberal sentiments and kind heart, they wished to put him upon the throne. If that conspiracy had been successful, he would have filled the throne as the most clement prince that Italy had. I have seen, sir, this old man walking with his hands behind his back, superintending the improvements at Leghorn, and other parts of his dominions, patting the little children on the head, talking to the working people, and nodding familiarly to the market-women—the very picture of a good king. Has this man changed? Yes. At that very time the minions of the Pope endeavored to use him in oppressing the people; but he put them one side, and set his face against the influence of religious tyranny. But he has now grown old, his brain has become weak, his heart fearful, and he has changed. It is not the Grand Duke of Tuscany now, it is the priest. Am I wrong in charging this upon the priesthood? The Pope is a priest, and the Pope is supreme at Rome. Let the Pope decree religious liberty—let the Pope wash his hands of religious oppression, let religion be free in Rome, and then shall I believe that religious oppression is not the act of the priest, but of the government.

But this very night there is within the city of Rome, a narrow street, with a gate at each end, into which is crammed every night from seven to eight hundred human beings. Drive through that street in the day-time, and you need perfume to keep you from fainting, such is the consequence of this dense population. Who are these people? They are almost under the shadow of the Vatican. And this most Christian sovereign of the most Christian Church has the power to set them free, but he closes the gates upon them at 8 o'clock every evening in winter, and 9 o'clock in the summer, and opens them in the morning at a corresponding hour. Why is this? Because they are Jews, and the Roman Catholic religion tolerates no religion but its own. If we are guilty of slander—if it seems like calumny to charge oppression upon those who profess in some respects the same faith as ourselves, let them wash their hands of these things. The Pope ought to be the champion of religious freedom. He should set the example to the world by allowing truth to come into contact with error.

If there be a city next to Jerusalem itself, filled with consecrated recollections, it is Rome—Rome, whose grounds are honey-combed with the tombs of early martyrs. A little while since, when there was danger, what did you see? A sovereign Prince, the representative of the Apostle—puts on a livery and gets behind a travelling carriage, and flies like a lackey! The coward fled! And he whose voice of authority had roared like a bull from the Vatican, roared from the palace of Gæta, like a petted calf!

Are you here to sympathize with a gentleman, a nobleman? This man who is imprisoned is what is called a *lackey*, a hired servant. This man, when called to give up his Bible, did he fly? fly like a Pope? No; superstition has made a Pope a coward, while the Bible has raised a lackey to the dignity of a nobleman.

He now called upon the priests to join in maintaining civil liberty. But he believed, if they controlled the municipal authorites of this city, as they do the Duke of Tuscany, his head to-morrow morning would not be worth a six-pence. And yet, said he, I here declare before God, that I hope I have the spirit of my country's history, and have drunk deeply enough of the spirit of religious liberty, to lay my head upon a block, and have it chopped off, before a single hair of the head of the most bigotted Papist in this land should suffer the least harm by religious persecution. [Here the audience broke out in the most uncontrollable applause, and the speaker took his seat.]

The Rev. S. H. Cox, D. D. of Brooklyn, N. Y. made the last address, which was highly appropriate and well received, but very short, in consequence of the lateness of the hour.

Having adopted the resolutions offered by a for mal vote, the meeting was dissolved by pronouncing the Apostolic Benediction.

Never before in this country was any religious meeting so distinguished, by the presence of so many persons of talent, piety, and influence, in the various walks of life. Its object was benevolent and Christian, and all except the bigotted Papist, infatuated and blinded by his false religion, were happy in being called to attend its solemnities. Popish priests, and others in connection with them, opposed it, and sought to disturb its hallowed proceedings, and to destroy the accomplishment of its end. But the effort was unavailing.—It went onward to its close in the happiest form, and its salutary influence soon began to show itself all over the land.

In Newark, N. J. a similar public meeting of great interest was held on Thursday evening, the 20th of January, at which the Mayor of the city, the Honorable Mr. Quimby, presided. Excellent addresses were delivered, and appropriate resolutions were adopted.

In Baltimore also, a great and enthusiastic meeting in behalf of religious liberty was held on the evening of the 19th of February following, at which it was computed that there were present at least, four thousand people, when the subject was discussed with great ability, and important resolutions were adopted.

By the Legislature of the State of New York the following resolutions were adopted, viz:

Resolutions of the New-York Legislature.

Resolved, (If the Assembly concur) That the Legislature of the State of New-York have regarded with deep solicitude and regret the recent persecutions to which Francesco Madiai, and his wife Rosa Madiai have been subjected in the Kingdom of Tuscany, for the alleged crime of reading the Holy Scriptures.

Resolved, (If the Assembly concur) That the congratulations with which the State of New York, formally and by public act, hailed, in 1847, the efforts of Pius IX, to ameliorate the condition of the Italian people, and to bestow upon them the incalculable blessing of national independence and constitutional freedom, make eminently proper at this time a formal and public remonstrance against cruel and flagrant oppression in the same land.

Resolved, (If the Assembly concur) That the President of the United States be respectfully requested to exert his best influence with the government of Tuscany to obtain, as a favor asked by a people which welcomes all strangers and protects all religions, permission for the Madiai, and their fellow-prisoners for the same offence, to emigrate to this country.

Resolved, (If the Assemby concur) That a copy of these resolutions be duly authenticated and forwarded by the Governor to the President of the United States, and to each of the Senators and Representatives in Congress from this State.

Meanwhile the subject reaches the Congress of the United States which was then in session, and was brought before the Senate by the Honorable Lewis Cass, and the House of Representatives by the Honorable Mr. Wilcox, particularly in its relation to American citizens, while residing or sojourning in foreign lands: and a few days before its adjournment the Honorable J. R. Underwood, Chairman of the Committee on Foreign Relations, at the close of an able Report upon it, submitted the following Resolutions to the Senate, and recommended their adoption, viz:—

RESOLUTIONS OF THE SENATE.

"*Resolved*, That it would be just and wise, on the part of the Government of the United States, in future treaties with foreign nations, to secure, if practicable, to our citizens residing abroad, the right of worshipping God, freely and openly, according to the dictates of their own consciences, by providing that 'they shall not be disturbed, molested, or annoyed in any manner, on account of their religious belief, nor in the proper exercise of their peculiar religion, either within their own private houses, or in churches, chapels, or other places appointed for public worship; and that they shall be at liberty to build and maintain places of worship in convenient situations, interfering in no way with, but respecting, the religion and customs of the country in which they reside.

"*Resolved further*, That it would be just and wise, in our future treaties with foreign nations, to secure to our citizens residing abroad the right to purchase and own burial-places, and to bury any of our citizens, dying abroad, in such places, with those religious ceremonies and observances deemed appropriate by the surviving relatives and friends of the deceased."

Before closing this chapter, the reader should be informed that at an early day the attention of the Honorable Millard Filmore, the President of the United States, had been called to the case of the Madiai, by a Committee appointed for that purpose in the city of New-York, and his influence solicited, so far as the duties of his office would permit; and a letter was consequently soon dispatched by the Honorable Mr. Everitt, the Secretary of State, to the Grand Duke of Tuscany, asking their release. It can hardly fail, though *unofficial*, to receive a respectful consideration; and it may be followed by the restoration of those pious people to their homes, or at least, by a permission to leave Tuscany and come to this country.

CHAPTER II.

Archbishop Hughes' Letter.

The meeting whose proceedings and some of its effects are noticed in the preceding chapter necessarily bore with considerable severity upon the Popish *system* of religion, and exposed its intolerant and persecuting spirit. The cause which the friends and advocates of that system chose to pursue, in regard to the meeting and the objects of it, demonstrated more clearly than it had been done in this country before, that these traits attach to the American branch of the establishment, as really as to the European. Romanists, in common with all other citizens, were invited to attend and to give their influence against religious intolerance, and in favor of religious freedom. They did not comply with the invitation. They withheld all cooperation, and in the way of lectures, sermons, and newspaper articles, simultaneously put forth throughout the country in large numbers, misrepresenting the whole matter, and vindicating the action of the Grand Duke, in his treatment of the Madiai, sought to embarrass, if not to break down and destroy the good influences which the friends of religious freedom had set in motion.

Various pens had ably corrected many of the misrepresentations that had been made by Popish Priests, lecturers, correspondents and editors, when the Archbishop of New-York, the Rev. John Hughes, D. D. deemed it necessary to bring the weight of his personal influence, and the power of his reasoning to bear upon the matter, that the attention of the public might be diverted from the real question at issue, and the Popish operations in this land still be undisturbed, and the true character of Popery be saved from, at least, a hazardous exposure. Therefore on the 18th of February, six weeks after the meeting in the Metropolitan Hall, the following letter from him, though addressed to the Freeman's Journal, was published in the New-York Daily Times. The next day it appeared in the New-York Herald, and also in the Freemans' Journal to which latter it was addressed. It is a remarkable document, and shows to what extremes one may be led against humanity, courtesy, reason and truth, when committed by vows to a false system of religion and politics, as is the system of Popery. The reader will see that it counts very largely on the ignorance, credulity, and forbearance, of the American people; and shows an indifference to facts, and a willingness to mislead, which are sadly at variance with moral uprightness. Here it is.

"To the Editor of the New-York Freemans' Journal."

"The heading of this communication suggests the matter which it proposes to discuss. No preface or introduction is necessary. The case of the Madiai, as reported in newspapers, had already attracted the attention and active sympathy of distinguished gentlemen, especially in England, previous to its having been taken up in this country. It had been the occasion of meetings at Exeter Hall in London. It had been especially adopted by Sir Culling Eardley and Lord Roden, who are by no means distinguished as promoters of religious liberty in their own country. Under such sanction in England it would be strange if the movement did not produce some corresponding action in this country. For latterly it seems as if the philanthropists of this land deem it their highest honor to be imitators of the corresponding class in England. There is nothing done by the aristocracy of England in the name of benevolence and philanthropy, which does not immediately provoke the desire of imitation among the aristocracy here. And the only example that we have failed to imitate is the establishment of Ragged Schools, which have become so popular in London and its vicinity. This we have not ventured on, although Heaven knows, so far as the title is concerned, the materials are not wanting. England, as an accompaniment of the emigration of at least her Catholic subjects, has not allowed them to leave her shores unprovided with all the requisites fitting them for admission into Ragged Schools.

"With this exception, whatever becomes popular among a certain class of English nobility and gentry is sure to be imitated on this side of the ocean. In this way we can account for the convocation of a Madiai sympathy meeting at Metropolitan Hall. The call of the meeting was signed by some of our most respectable citizens. It was attended by a very large assemblage of persons who would attend the meetings of Exeter Hall against Catholics with as much sympathy and pleasure. The proceedings of the meeting were in strict accordance with its purpose, which was to shut off all free discussion, and to excite an unkind, uncharitable, and bitter Protestant feeling against the Catholics of the United States and of the world. I should perhaps observe in this place, to the credit of the Protestant clergy of this City, that if they attended the meeting at all, it was only in the capacity of silent spectators—while the resolutions were brought forward, and speeches delivered by reverend brethren imported apparently for the occasion, from the suburban and neighboring villages around New-York.

"I need not refer to the course which was given to the whole discussion on that occasion. I may remark, however, that it comprised a scurrilous denunciation of the Grand Duke of Tuscany, of the Jesuits, of the Pope, of Catholic Governments in Europe, of the Catholic citizens of the United States, and of the Catholic religion and its members of all times and places. This was the purpose to which the Madiai meeting directed its powers of eloquence and denunciation. Whether the gentlemen who signed the call for that meeting, Hon. Luther Bradish, Collector Hugh Maxwell, Hiram Ketchum, Esq., and other gentlemen of equal respectability, intended to furnish an occasion for denouncing their Catholic fellow-citizens in this country, is more than I can take upon me to decide. From my previous knowledge of some of these gentlemen, and my respect for all, I should be unwilling to believe that they would loan their honored names for a purpose so unworthy of their social position, and so much at variance with the civil institutions of their country. I cannot, however, acquit them of responsibility in this—that having accepted, or assumed the trust of calling a public meeting, they delegated that trust to other trustees, in whom the public could not have the same confidence. Other meetings like that at Metropolitan Hall have already been held in other parts of the country, and the probability is, that Messrs. Bradish, Maxwell and Ketchum, whether it was their intention or not, will have inaugurated a Protestant crusade against their Catholic fellow-citizens hardly less violent, or less dishonorable, than that which resulted from the 'Awful Disclosures of Maria Monk.'

"The wisdom and expediency of giving any encouragement to religious excitements in connection with civil and social rights, appear to me extremely doubtful. The Catholics of this country have had nothing to do with the trial and the imprisonment of the Madiai in Florence. What good effect, therefore, will be produced by an attempt, through the medium of public meetings, to denounce them for an act which they had no power either to accomplish or prevent? Is it wise to encourage strifes among the various denominations of which the people of the United States are composed? Would it not be wiser to recognize the rights of such denomination and of each individual, fully and frankly, as they are recognized by the Constitution of the country? Some have the same right to be Catholics as others have to be Protestants. All have the right to profess what religion they please. And since this is the condition of all the people of the United States, is it wise or just to denounce any portion of them for the offences, real or imaginary, committed by their brethren of the same creed in foreign countries? The time may come, and perhaps sooner than is expected by our wisest public men, when the United States will have need of the support of all her citizens. Who can tell whether the future of this country may not reveal dangers either from foreign enemies or from internal divisions, which will test the loyalty and fidelity of every citizen, of whatever religion? In such an emergency the Catholics, in spite of the denunciations to which they have been lately exposed, will be found among the fastest friends of the Union and the bravest defenders of the soil. They have ever been such—and during the last few years, when even statesmen, not of their religion, were ready to follow the lead of a foreign demagogue, the Catholics have exhibited evidences of self-control, of calm and wise loyalty to the United States, of a well-poised self-possession which have entitled them to the respect of their countrymen. If it be true, then, that from the earliest colonization of these States, and through all the struggles which they had to undergo in peace or in war, the Catholics have ever sustained an untarnished reputation, have never furnished a coward on battle-field, or a traitor in council: if they have discharged honorably their civil duties in times of peace, and their obligations of patriotism in times of war, why should they now, under the auspices of the gentlemen who called the meeting at Metropolitan Hall, be given over to the coarse and vulgar denunciations of the reverend orators who figured on that occasion?

The charge alleged in the preamble of the resolutions adopted at that meeting, and on which the resolutions themselves are founded, is that *for no other crime* except that of 'possessing and reading their Bible,' the Madiai, husband and wife, were tried, convicted, and incarcerated by the Government of Tuscany: if this charge be the truth, the whole truth; and nothing but the truth; I am quite free and willing to denounce the proceedings of the Government of Tuscany as oppressive, unjust and cruel. Such an act would be a disgrace to any Government, Catholic or Protestant. But I must beg leave to say that I do not believe the truth of the charge. I regard it as a falsehood, and I have no doubt that it will turn out to be so. If this should prove to be the case, the proceedings at Metropolitan Hall will reflect but little credit on those who sanctioned and took part in them. Observe, I do not doubt the truth of the statement that the Madiai 'possessed and read their Bible,' but I do doubt and deny that for this *alone*, they were tried and condemned to prison. I must observe at the same time, that I have no knowledge of the circumstances of the case, except what has come under the notice of every one who has read the newspapers of the day concerning it. I have come to this conclusion on grounds of probability, which to my mind are not less strong in their aggregate than positive and direct testimony.

First—There is no law in Tuscany against 'possessing and reading the Bible.' *Second*—Even if there was such a law, it is impossible that the Madiai should have been convicted under it, inasmuch as, in their very prison, they are allowed to 'possess and read their Bible.' It is not probable that any country would punish an offender for a crime, and yet allow them to continue, during the penalty, in the commission of the same. For instance, in our own courts, men convicted of forgery are not allowed to carry on the trade in the State's Prison. I think that these reflections will satisfy any candid mind that the Madiai are not condemned *solely*, for the crime of 'possessing and reading the Bible.' And if they are not condemned *solely* for this, it follows that the proceedings at Metropolitan Hall are founded on positive falsehood. This circumstance, however, was not thought worthy of consideration, and the truth would have been rather a detriment than an advantage to the purpose of the meeting. The impression intended to be made by the speakers on that occasion was that the Government of Tuscany, the Jesuits, the Pope, and the members of the Catholic Church throughout the world have a mortal dread of the Bible. This would be strange indeed. To them, the book, the New Testament at least, was originally given in manuscript by its inspired authors. They have been its witnesses and its guardians from the beginning. It has been recognized and used by them as, in so far as it goes, a duplicate in parchment of the doctrines which our Saviour had inscribed with a pencil of divine fire in characters of living faith on the heart of the Church. The art of printing facilitated its diffusion, and the Church availed herself, with eagerness, of that art for the purpose of multiplying copies of the Holy Scriptures. Numerous editions of the Bible were published in the principal languages of Europe under the patronage of Popes, Cardinals and Bishops, long before Protestantism came into being. The Italians were well acquainted with the Bible in their own beautiful language before Martin Luther was born. The first Italian edition was published in Venice in the year 1471, and forty successive editions were published in the different cities of Italy anterior to the date of the Protestant translation which was published, not in Italy, but in Geneva, in the year 1562. In the very year of American Independence the Arch-bishop of Florence brought out another translation, for which he received the special thanks of Pope Pius VI. In our own country, the Catholics have published not less than twenty or twenty-five editions of the Holy Scripture, of every size, from the folio down to the octavo, many of which are stereotyped. Is it not surprising then that our Protestant neighbors will persist in supposing that we are afraid of our own original and hereditary documents that have never been out of our possession!

Connected with the case of the Madiai, a new national policy has been broached in the Senate of the United States, by no less distinguished a Senator than General Cass. This policy, with which the gentlemen at Metropolitan Hall appeared to be very familiar, purports to us a vindication of the rights of conscience, to be secured to all American citizens, in whatever countries they may choose to travel or sojourn. The ground on which this policy is advanced is that in this country strangers of every nation are allowed to exercise their religion as their conscience may dictate, and therefore in all other countries Americans have the right to claim and exercise a similar privilege. It is hardly necessary for me to observe that freedom of conscience which is here contended for is inviolable in its very nature and essence. To say that any man or any nation has either physical or moral power to destroy freedom of conscience, is to give utterance to a patent absurdity. Conscience without freedom is not conscience, but for this very reason the freedom of conscience is beyond the reach of man's power. God has provided in the human soul a fortress to which it can retreat, and from which it can hurl defiance against all invaders. I presume, therefore, that there is a confusion of ideas in the minds of those who, with Gen. Cass, plead eloquently for that which requires no pleading, namely, freedom of conscience.

That is universal—that is indestructible—that is inviolable. They must be understood to mean liberty of external action according to conscience, which is quite a different thing. This external liberty of action, according to conscience, in all countries, is regulated to a certain extent by the enactment of positive laws. In some countries the range is wider, in others more restricted; but it is limited in all, not even excepting the United States. The liberty of conscience which is recognized and applauded in Connecticut will not be tolerated (on certain subjects) in South Carolina or in Alabama. The Mormons have been obliged to seek retirement in Deseret in order to enjoy what they call liberty of conscience. And the liberty which they there enjoy would not be allowed them under the toleration of the laws of New-York. Is it expected then, in the project of Gen. Cass, that they, too, shall have the privilege of exercising liberty of conscience in their peregrinations among foreign States!

Again, the assumption of General Cass is a fallacy. He assumes that the freedom of religion in this country is a *boon*, conceded by Protestant liberality to all the inhabitants of the land. This is not so. It is a privilege which was won by the good swords of Catholics and Protestants in the battles for National Independence. It is a common right, therefore, and is not to be regarded as a concession from one to the other. This arrangement, in regard to liberty of conscience, suited the policy of the country, and was absolutely indispensable after the revolutionary war. Does General Cass mean to say, that because it suited us, all other nations must adopt it, whether it suits them or not? As well might England say, that because it suited her finances to adopt Free Trade, she will insist upon it that all other nations shall do the same. Gen. Cass knows as well as any man living, that until this country becomes vastly stronger, and foreign States much weaker than they are, all pleadings on this subject will be treated as drivelling by foreign States. Oh, if you have a mind to arrange the constitutions and laws of European States by the power of armies and navies, that indeed is another matter. But the United States will expose themselves to ridicule if they drag in such a question into their diplomatic intercourse with foreign governments.

It is a recognised principle in this country that every sovereign and independent nation has the right to adopt its own constitution and laws. The constitution and laws of a country are but the aggregate of general principles applicable to the peculiar situation, protection and welfare of the citizens or subjects of which it is composed. They may be regarded as the public and permanent expression of the *aggregate conscience* of that State. Thus, without going out of our own country, Massachusetts has one form of public conscience, Louisiana has another. Does Mr.

Cass mean to say that an obolitionist from Boston, under the plea of liberty of conscience, still has the right to talk in New Orleans, and preach, and harangue, and write, and publish, on the subject of Slavery as he might choose to do in Faneuil Hall? If not, I would say, with all respect, that the policy in regard to this subject, which General Cass advocates in the Senate, is calculated to have no practical effect, either at home or abroad, except to stir up sectarian animosities against his Catholic fellow-citizens, and this is hardly worthy of his patriotic services, advanced age, or accumulated honors.

Indeed, I am quite persuaded that the country has lowered itself in dignity, if it be true, as the newspapers have stated, that the President, through Secretary Everett, has become a petitioner, side by side with Lord Roden, and taken his place of expectation and hope in the ante-chamber of the Grand Duke of Tuscany. The supreme government of this country ought not to stoop to an investigation, however sacred may be the occasion, of a political trial in the petty States of Italy. In doing so, it exposes itself to humiliation and rebuke without redress. The Grand Duke can easily ask Mr. Secretary Everett certain questions about the liberty of conscience in this country, which the latter would find himself exceedingly puzzled to answer. If the Grand Duke or his Minister should ask Mr. Everett whether liberty of conscience is recognized in the United States as unlimited—the same in one State as in another—the Secretary will have to reply, "No." If the same interrogator should ask Mr. Everett what became of the helpless female inmates of a certain Convent in Charlestown, near Boston, who were driven out without accusation, or trial, or condemnation before any civil tribunal; expelled from their peaceful home in the depths of night, their house and furniture committed to the flames. Can Mr. Everett tell what happened to them afterwards? Again the Secretary would have to answer, "No." Did the State of Massachusetts make any compensation to these persons for the destruction of their property, or the violation of their rights? Mr. Everett would have to answer, "No." Is the State of Massachusetts bound to protect the individual rights of her citizens? Mr. Everett would have to answer, "Yes," in theory; in practice, in this case, at least, "No." How, then, it might further be asked, do you pretend that liberty of conscience is extended to all the citizens of the United States? Is there any practical difference between the social intolerance which prevails in your country, where there are so many religions, and the legal intolerance of our dominions, where there is but one? It seems to me that the Secretary of the United States, who has it not in his power to give different answers to questions such as these, rather exposes himself and his native State, if not his country, by going all the way to Florence to plead for liberty of conscience, while such violations of its rights have been perpetrated and left unrecompensed at his own door. Other violations of liberty of conscience in different parts of the country are by no means rare in our history. They occurred in Philadelphia, where churches and convents were burned to ashes by the intolerance of the mob. There is this, however, to be said in extenuation, that at least, if the civil authorities of Pennsylvania did not protect its citizens from these outrages, it allowed compensation for the damage done to their property. I fear much that social intolerance is not to be ascribed so much to the principles of any religion, as to the diseased moral nature which is the common inheritance of us all. The evidence of this can be discovered no less in the United States than elsewhere. There is among us a superabundance of social and domestic intolerance, in despite of those laws of religious freedom of which we are so ready to boast, but which unfortunately have no power to protect the object of that intolerance. Is it rare that poor servants are driven out from their employment, because they will not, against their conscience, join the domestic religion "of State," which the family has made exclusive? Is it unusual to hear of men disinheriting their own offspring for no cause except that of practising their acknowledged rights of conscience? These are matters with which we are made too familiar, notwithstanding our boasted rights and liberty of conscience.

I have offered these remarks not in any spirit of controversy, but in the spirit of peace and of truth. There are moments when every citizen who feels that he can say something, promotive of the welfare of his countrymen, and of advantage to his country, is authorized to give public utterance to his sentiments, however humble soever he may be. With such a feeling, I offer the foregoing reflections to the consideration of my fellow-citizens for what they are worth—no more.

† JOHN, Archbishop of New-York.

Replies to Archbishop Hughes.

CHAPTER III.

Mr. Phelps' Letter.

In America it would be ruinous to Popery and the prospects of its Priesthood to have their hostility to the people's possession, and use of the Bible, generally known. To conceal this hostility, the chief cause of the persecution of the Madiai was an important object in the Archbishop's letter; and the language employed in it was so artfully arranged as to imply that the Papacy had always cherished the Scriptures, and amply provided for their general distributions, and that no obstacle existed to their unrestricted circulation and use in Italy at the pre sent time. Therefore, on the 23d of February, five days after its publication, the following letter, addressed to the Archbishop by the gentleman whose name it bears, was published in various newspapers in the city of New-York, and also in a number of other cities of the United States. But it failed to procure from him, or any of the authorities of the Papal church, the desired information—and this failure, on their part, must necessarily be regarded as a cautioned acknowledgement that the Bible can NOT be distributed among, and read by the people in Italy, with the approbation of the Papal powers. But we subjoin the letter:—

"*The Madiai Meeting at Metropolitan Hall.*

"To Rev. Archbishop Hughes:

"SIR,—As one of the Committee engaged in making arrangements for the 'Madiai Meeting' in Metropolitan Hall, I beg leave to call attention to a statement in your letter, that the occasion was made use of 'to denounce our Catholic fellow-citizens in this country;' 'to inaugurate a Protestant crusade against our Catholic fellow-citizens.' Reports of all the speeches made on the occasion are easily accessible, and prove that anything more false than this accusation was never stated by any authority, clerical or laical. The principal speakers used nothing but the kindest and most respectful language in regard to our Catholic fellow-citizens, and urged them to join with us in denouncing and petitioning against all such outrageous tyranny and injustice as that practiced upon this poor family, for conscience sake. Every honorable man, of the thousands present at the meeting, will testify to this fact, and it will require something more than your bare assertion to convince the intelligent and respectable of your own community of its falsity.

"It is true that a good deal of laughter was excited by the extracts read by one of the speakers from your unfortunate lecture on the subject of 'Civil and Religious Freedom,' delivered in the same Hall; but it was all in good humor, and at your expense.

"In regard to your statement that 'the art of printing facilitates the diffusion of the Holy Scriptures, and that the Church avails herself with eagerness of that art for the purpose of multiplying copies of them,' we beg leave to ask you which translation of the Holy Scriptures into the Italian language is acceptable to the Church, and sure to meet with the 'patronage of Popes, Cardinals and Bishops?' and we pledge ourselves to print a large edition of this translation, and send it to Italy for gratuitous distribution. We wait anxiously a reply to this inquiry, as our offer is made in perfect good faith, and we shall be glad to get your guarantee against the pecuniary risks of our enterprise.

"ANSON G. PHELPS, JR."

Reply by an Officer of the Amer. & For. Christian Union.

The unmistakable evidence of sympathy on the part of the Popish Priests, in this country, with the Grand Duke of Tuscany, and their approbation of his oppressive acts, gave a new view of Popery, and its spirit, to many Americans, and forced deep and abiding convictions upon them in regard to it, which, previously, they had not entertained. In consequence of this the letter of the Archbishop received a more general attention than would otherwise have been given to it; and several replies of an interesting character touching different parts were published, in different places. The following, exposing its misrepresentations and sophistries, is more full than was warranted by the objects which the writer of the preceding one had in view; and was published on the 2d of March, one week later, in the New-York Daily Times, one of the journals through which the Archbishop had given his communication to the public. If it is severe, it is so by reason of its truthfulness.

The Archbishop has not answered the calls made on him in it; and his silence is necessarily regarded as an acknowledgment of his inability to make good some of his affirmations, or to defend the positions he had taken. But we subjoin the letter:

To the Rev. John Hughes,
Roman Catholic Archbishop of New York,

DEAR SIR,—In your remarkable letter of the

18th inst. upon the subject 'of the Madiai meeting,' held in the Metropolitan Hall, in this city, in January last, and 'the proceedings in the United States,' you say: 'There are moments when every citizen who feels that he can say something promotive of the welfare of his countrymen, and of advantage to his country, is authorized to give public utterance to his sentiments, however humble he may be;' and you offer it in justification of what you had then written. You will accept it, I trust, as my justification in addressing to you the present communication.

I have read your letter attentively, and cannot but regret that you were induced by any consideration whatever to send it forth into the community, conveying, as it does, the impression that you regard its sentiments as verities, and the belief of them, to be promotive of the welfare of the people. For, with all impartial readers, it must necessarily affect their estimate both of your head and your heart, very unhappily; and also do much to destroy the hope which many had of late entertained, in regard to the Church of which you are an honored minister, and in regard to yourself as a friend of religious freedom, according to statements from your pen made not a great while ago.

"It was hoped that the progress of the Nineteenth Century, in literature, arts, science, and civilization, had produced many and important changes in the dogmas and practices of the Roman Catholic Church; and especially, that the intolerance which distinguished it in the 'dark ages' had given place to what was more worthy of the Christian name. But the spirit of your letter, the things you have chosen to say, and the manner in which you have executed the whole document, make it quite certain that it is vain to hope, in regard either to yourself as an American citizen, or in regard to Roman Catholicism as a religion, adapted to do good to this or any other land.

"No one, on reading your letter, can avoid the conviction, that you descend from your high position, and duties as a minister of religion, who should 'study the things which make for peace,' to do the work which, if uncorrected by other hands, must result in strifes, and hatreds, and divisions, and other evils. But it is to be hoped that your movements and Romanism too, will be understood, and that what now *seems* to be your purpose, will be thwarted.

"You sneer at England, in the reference you make to her 'aristocracy,' 'nobility,' and 'gentry,'—and your rudeness, not to say insult, to Americans in the affirmation that, in their movements to promote benevolent objects they are merely 'imitators of the English aristocracy,' might perhaps have been expected from a Roman Catholic less enlightened than yourself, and in the heat of controversy—but they were not to have been expected from you. They are, however, deliberately put forth, and they seem *designed* to create and to foster unhappy feelings. England, I know, indeed, has declared for, and defended the rights of conscience, the unrestricted circulation and use of the Holy Bible, and constitutional Government, too firmly, and faithfully, to hope for favor from Romanists in Continental Europe, or in any Roman Catholic country ; but you are in the United States, the land of Liberty, and it was natural to expect you to give your influence, whatever it might be, to the cause of freedom, and also that you would treat with decency and respect all your fellow citizens. But we are disappointed.

"There is no 'aristocracy' known in America ; and yet you speak of such a class as actually existing here, and you affirm, that the 'call of the meeting' originated in a disposition to 'imitate the English Aristocracy.' This representation is very unhappy. The meeting was *not* called in connexion with the meetings held in Europe on the subject, nor in consequence of them. It was called by reason of the claims which suffering humanity urged, and also which members of the Christian Church, imprisoned by a tyrant, simply for reading the Bible, have on the sympathy and kind offices of all Christians. The meeting was purely American in its origin, and in everything that distinguished it.

"But suppose it was called in 'imitation' of what had been done in England. Is 'a philanthropic and benevolent object less valuable because Englishmen may have moved *first* in regard to it? Certainly not. Your philosophy is defective; and your sneer and mis-statements are not convincing. If an object is worthy, no matter what nation or people move first in promoting it, all should seek to advance it by all the means in their power.

"But it is particularly painful to see you forget the proprieties of your position, and of Christian character upon so small a matter as the non-establishment, in this country, of what are termed in England "Ragged Schools,' and appeal, in the flippant manner you do, to God, whose name we are forbidden 'to take in vain.' Why should you become excited? Do you desire their establishment, and the introduction of 'grades' and 'classes' among our people? I know it is thought by some, that your sympathies for the peculiarities of European Governments are of late grown very strong; but these should not lead you to *such* use as you make of the name of God. It savors more of the feelings and manners of the irreligious and profane, than of those of the pious, and especially of a Teacher of religion. You say that you wrote 'for the welfare of your countrymen and the advantage of your country;' but these cannot be promoted by such examples of profaneness in the ministers of religion. If, therefore, you have occasion to write again, I beg you to be more careful in this respect. Rude and uncalled for appeals to

'Heaven,' add nothing to the weight and influence of an argument, while their omission is much more becoming the pen and heart of one who is invested with the office of an Archbishop.

"But I must call your attention to your affirmations respecting what you call the 'purpose of the meeting,' and its 'proceedings.' You affirm that 'the purpose of the meeting' was 'to shut off all free discussion, and to excite an unkind, uncharitable and bitter Protestant feeling against the Catholics of the United States and of the world.' You say, also, 'the proceedings were in strict accordance with the purpose.'

"In making these affirmations you doubtless understood your position, and you will, if called upon, demonstrate their truth; or, failing to do it, consent to be regarded as a slanderer. We are constrained to call on you for proof; for we must and do deny your statements to be true. The 'purpose' of the meeting was as expressed in the 'Call.' It was 'to express sympathy for the suffering Madiai, and to devise measures for their relief;' and this was the controling idea of the occasion, as thousands of the most reliable persons who were present will testify. 'The proceedings' were *not* as you represent them to have been; but, on the contrary, the rights and privileges of Romanists were pleaded for, and the defence of them, against all usurpation and tyranny, pledged by the meeting with as much earnestness and good feeling as were those of the Protestants; and you, and all Romanists in the community were kindly and earnestly called upon, to unite with us in this effort to advance the cause of religious freedom. You made no favorable response. You refused to coöperate in so humane and noble a work; but a representative of your denomination who, during the progress of the meeting occupied himself, at times, in 'hissing' and in other unworthy exercises, was put forward to disturb, and, if possible, to break it up and to destroy its good effects. How many were associated with him, and placed in various parts of the Hall ready to act at a given signal, I do not know. It is sufficient for me to know that the effort was ineffectual. The plan did not succeed.

"And why do you now complain, and berate the conductors of that meeting, as though some wrong had been inflicted by them on you, or on Roman Catholics? If you are a friend of religious freedom, you were invited to attend the meeting, in common with all others. Did you attend? If not—why not? If you were present in the Hall, as some say you were, why did you not come forward, when a kind public invitation was given to you, and thus prove your friendship to the cause, and also, to the unrestricted circulation and use of the Holy Scriptures? But I will not urge you to answer, why. An answer might force you to tell a terrible truth, which millions, in this land, are now beginning to believe, by reason of the course which you, and other leaders of the Roman Catholic Church, are pursuing. It might force you to say that you are a Jesuit, and the subject of a foreign Prince, who has nothing more at heart than the embarrassment of our Republic, in which men are encouraged to act and to think for themselves,—and further, that you are bound, by vows you have taken, to carry out the 'Instructions,' received from that Prince to promote Romanism, whatever may become of all other interests. This would be a terrible confession; but still, if you were governed by the truth, you might possibly have to make it. Would it not be so? Many do more than suspect it.

"But when you wrote your letter, you *probably* would have answered as to your nonattendance, by saying, that you did *not* believe that the Madiai were imprisoned for 'reading the Scriptures.' You said so then. But you will hardly say it now, because it cannot be supposed that you failed to read, in the New-York *Herald* of the 19th inst. a full report of the trial, derived from Italian sources, which was printed by the side of your letter, and which confirmed the popular opinion on the subject, and exposed, in a number of instances, the misrepresentations which your letter contained. But this report contained no facts that we had not from *reliable sources* before. Your refusal to coöperate, seems to involve more than unbelief.

"You are doubtless right, in saying that 'the Roman Catholics, in this country, had nothing to do with the trial and imprisonment of the Madiai;' and had they been 'denounced on account of it,' you would have been right in proposing, as you do, the inquiry: Whether any good could result from denouncing them in public meetings, for an act which they had not power, either to accomplish or prevent?' But they were *not* denounced, and your insinuation is highly improper, indeed morally wrong, and unless you can make the truth of it to appear, it must react upon yourself very disadvantageously. The community must entertain such notions of your honor and truthfulness, as are forced upon them by the course you pursue.

"I do not deny that the system of the Roman Catholic religion, and its Hierarchy, are denounced in America, and of late with much more severity than formerly; because its unscriptural character, and oppressive tendencies, are now more openly avowed, and better understood; but the *Laity*, who have been deluded by the System and its Priesthood, have not been denounced. On the contrary, they have shared largely in the sympathies of American Protestants, who in a great variety of ways have proved their kindness of feeling towards them, and their readiness to afford them relief; and I am happy to be able to inform you, that very many Roman Catholics have availed themselves of this friendly disposition, and are now happy in the enjoyment of Protestant freedom. Multitudes more, we trust, will soon imitate their example, and enjoy like happiness.

"But to another point;—your apparent painful anxiety, that 'religion' should be separated from 'civil and social rights;' and that everything adapted to alienate the various denominations in the country should be avoided; because the entire strength of the nation, as you intimate, may, at some future day, be needed for its protection. That 'the future of this country may reveal dangers from foreign enemies;' and the influences of some who consent to be their tools, though they dwell with us and have the favor of citizenship, no intelligent person, who has carefully observed the course of things for some years past, perhaps, entertains a doubt. But it seems strange to those who have observed your course, and that of other leaders in the Roman Catholic ranks, that you should venture to read a homily to the American Protestant community on this topic. What a pity you had not thought of this grave matter before, and taken 'the beam from your own eye before you attempted to take the mote' from the eyes of Protestants! It would have saved a vast amount of outlay, on the part of Roman Catholics, in the form of Lyceums, Institutes, Public

Lectures, impassioned orations, newspaper articles, 'circulars' from Councils, and such like things, by which it has been sought to bring Roman Catholics into direct and bitter antagonism with other classes of citizens. It would have prevented also that violent onset that is now made by Roman Catholics in all sections of the United States against our common school system, and also that bitterness of feeling which manifests itself against various American institutions, and Americans themselves, in the coarse and vulgar threats with which, at least, some Roman Catholic periodicals are partially filled. When reading us this homily on cultivating kind and respectful feelings, and doing 'the things which make for peace' and unity in the land, had you forgotten your own course? Or did you suppose that Protestants had forgotten it? They cannot forget it so easily. And I will venture to predict, that if the course which you and your associates have pursued on these matters, for some time past, is *not* abandoned, and substituted by one *more kind and respectful to public sentiment and feeling, and the laws of the land*, you will, for yourselves and your denomination, destroy that respect and good feeling which others desire to cherish towards you. You may in time occasion the rise throughout this country, which is sacred to liberty—civil and religious—of a Protestant party, with a view to vindicate and sustain American principles, and our legalized and valued institutions, against Roman Catholic violence and abuse. It is earnestly hoped that you will not press matters to this result. Protestants, I am sure, do not desire such a result. But if it should take place, and bear with considerable oppressiveness upon Roman Catholics, American Protestants will be free from the responsibility of causing it. On Romanists the responsibility will rest.

"But what you have said about the Bible, and the views and usages of the Roman Catholic Church in regard to its circulation and use by the people, should be received with considerable allowance.

"Your claim to antiquity as a church, and to have received the original manuscripts of the New Testament from the hands of their inspired authors, is ridiculous enough, as authentic history assures us that your church had no existence till after the lapse of centuries from the times of the Apostles.

"It did not rise till the spirit of Anti-Christ, which began to discover itself while the Apostles were present, had had time, through apostacies and various corruptions of the doctrines and institutions of Christianity, to furnish the materials, and an opportunity for its formation. Then it rose in an organized form, but it was too late, by several hundreds of years, to receive anything from the hands of *divinely* inspired writers.

"What you say about the printing of various editions of the Bible in Europe, is very well so far as it goes. But it misleads because more is not said by you. To give the true impression, you should have added that these books were restricted to a narrow circulation by the enormous prices at which they were held; and also that those only might have them who could obtain, from the Roman Catholic Priest, a written permission to that effect. The possession of a Bible by a person therefore does not depend, in a Roman Catholic country, on a desire to have it, nor simply an ability to pay for it; but on the judgment or caprice of a Priest, who has the control of the matter.

"What, then, is this but a *practical* withholding of the Bible from the people, by church authority, notwithstanding the parade you have made of the fact, that the Roman Catholic Church has printed various editions and versions of the Scriptures in Europe? It is, notwithstanding, withholding the Bible from the people; and in all Roman Catholic countries it is proverbially true that the masses of the people do not have the Scriptures. The large and costly editions they cannot buy if they would, in case the Priest would permit them to do it; and the cheaper editions, furnished by Bible Societies, they are forbidden to receive, 'on pain of excommunication,' and of ruin both for this life and the life that is to come. These things you will not venture to deny in sight of the enactments of the Council of Trent, which are authoritative in your Communion, and of the 'Official Bulls' issued within forty years past by Pius VII. Leo XII. Pius VIII. and Gregory XVI.

"That the Bible should be printed by you in America is not strange, however hostile your church may be to its free circulation, for America is the land where the people honor the Bible as the great instrument in securing their distinguished prosperity and happiness. Opposition, therefore, to the Bible, professedly and openly made by you, would fatally affect your prospects and hopes of success in this land; and you are too wise not to suppress the expression of disapprobation of its free distribution, as you have suppressed, in the edition which you have approved for American use, such notes as would be sure to hinder your prosperity here, if made known to the public, though they are of canonical authority, and are published in the editions intended for circulation in Roman Catholic lands.

"In concluding your letter, you speak of a 'new national policy that has been broached in the Senate of the United States, in connection with the case of the Madiai,' and which you truly say, 'purports to be a vindication of the rights of conscience, to be secured to all American citizens, in whatever countries they may choose to travel or sojourn,' and it appears to meet your special disapprobation, although similar privileges are secured in this country to strangers from every nation of the world. You seem to endeavor, in various ways, to cloud the subject, and so to embarrass it as to hinder its favorable consideration by the people. But something more clear, as well as forcible, will probably be requisite in order to secure that result.

"You say that 'there is a confusion of ideas in the minds of those who, with General Cass, plead for freedom of conscience,' and you very kindly tell the world what they *would* say, if they only knew how. This is, indeed, very generous of you. But I have looked carefully at what you say about conscience and its freedom, and I am forced to believe that 'the confusion of ideas' is with yourself rather than with the friends of the measure contemplated.* With you, if I understand your reasoning on the subject, 'freedom of conscience' is the synonym of 'licentiousness.' But this is by no means the view of those who plead for its being secured to our citizens in every nation with which we may hereafter enter into any treaty; and the phrase will be understood in its

* You speak of "conscience" as an entity—as something having an existence distinct and separate from the human soul; for you say, "God has provided in the human soul a fortress, to which it can retreat, and from which it can hurl defiance against all invaders." What then is it? If it is something *outside* of the soul, which can, in time of need take refuge in "a fortress provided" for it in the soul—what is it? Is it part of our *physical* nature? Where does it belong? From the following sentence, which occurs in a subsequent paragraph of the discussion, where you speak of

true and proper sense; and the thing signified will be appreciated by the Protestants of this land, notwithstanding all your attempts to embarrass and prejudice it. And, I trust that the 'policy,' as you call it, in our national legislation, will prevail, and ever hereafter be maintained.

"Your statements in regard to some things in the early history of the United States, it is thought, need considerable modifications to conform them to the truth. With what seems to many an unbecoming assurance, you declare that in regard to them, 'the assumptions of General Cass are a fallacy.' You then set up a claim for Roman Catholics, as the founders of this Government, and the authors of its freedom in the same sense, and to the extent, which such claim should be accorded to Protestants. You put forth a similar claim once before. Then, perhaps, you might have been excusable, on the ground that you had not the means to know certainly that the claim was wholly groundless. But now this plea can

the laws of a country, viz: "They may be regarded as the public and permanent expression of the aggregate conscience of a State,"—I take it, that in your estimation, "conscience" and "will" are identical. For it is usual to consider and speak of the laws of a people, as the embodiment or exponent of their "will," on the topics to which the laws refer. But I may have failed to understand you. If, however, "conscience" and "will" with you mean the same thing, and if you represent, in this, the views of your Church, no wonder that Rome is intolerant without compunction.

hardly be made. That you may not fall into the error of affirming these things again, would it not be well to turn your attention to our history, as a nation, a little more carefully? If you have not time to read extensively, I would suggest that you at least read Mr. Polk's review of your Roman Catholic Chapter in the history of the United States, in which its numerous fallacies are clearly and satisfactorily demonstrated, and the true state of the case shown. Roman Catholics, as such, had little or nothing to do in devising and securing the liberties of this country.

"And here let me say, that I am surprised at what appears to be your notion of national honor and glory. You say, 'I am persuaded that the country has lowered itself in dignity, if it be true that the President, through the Secretary Everett, has become a petitioner side by side with Lord Roden,' to 'the Grand Duke of Tuscany.' In your judgment, then, the Government may not interpose its moral influence, in the way of a request that suffering innocence should be released, without lowering its dignity! I had heretofore thought that to do good, and to seek to promote the prevalence of righteousness everywhere, whether in nations or narrower circles, was praiseworthy and honorable to those who engaged in it. Sure I am, that the Bible teaches such a sentiment, whatever you, an Archbishop of Romanism, may hold to the contrary. If it would be unworthy and inglorious to seek, by moral means, which inflicts no wrong, to induce a Government which is grossly sinning against its helpless subjects to desist from its course; then I take it that the opposite of this meets your idea of dignity and national honor. So then you would have persecution to reign without an effort to check it! It would be the glory of nations to stand by, and hear the shrieks of the despairing, the groans of the dying, and the sobs of the bereaved, or otherwise wretched by reason of the oppressions of those in power in a country, and yet attempt nothing for their releif! This may suit you, sir, and possibly it may be in keeping with the Canons of your Church; but it is as unnatural and heartless as it is at variance with the Scriptures, and with every just sentiment of true national dignity and honor; but this is not your doctrine when a Roman Catholic is to be relieved. It is in the remembrance of some, that you asked our Government to interfere with England, to relieve a Romanist—did our dignity wane then?

"Before leaving this portion of your letter, it is due to say that, in point of ingenuity and adaption to the end for which it was designed, it falls not a whit below any other portion. The Catechism, which is offered to Mr. Everett with seeming fairness, but so as to misslead the incautious, and give you an air of triumph, and an opportunity to intimate that public opinion in this country is identical with the 'legalized intolerance' of Roman Catholic countries, is an entire evasion of the subject under discussion. 'Freedom of conscience' was the thing to be spoken about and illustrated; but you have substituted licentiousness, and spoken as though the rebukes it received a few years since by an insulted and outraged community in Charlestown and Philadelphia were acts of violence suffered by Romanists 'for conscience sake.' Those sufferings at the hands of the populace, on the occasions alluded to, were induced by Roman Catholics themselves, and the consequence of many and most aggravated acts of wickedness on their part. I have no apology to make for mobs, but when the causes of them are misrepresented in order to inflict a wrong on our national character, it is proper to offer a correction. If you are familiar with the history of those cases, you must be aware that I have now placed them in the true light, as to their causes.

"I do not deny the existence, to some extent, and in some individual cases, of religious bigotry in this country, among Protestants. It is a defect, and is to be deplored, wherever it obtains. But, I do deny that 'intolerance' obtains with them to the extent, and in the form, which your statements and illustration seem designed to affirm. The principles of 'religious freedom' are sacredly guarded and cherished by our people; and as no slight evidence of it, I might cite your own undisturbed state, while you preach, and write, harrangue, and publish, and say and do so many things which are so entirely at variance with public sentiment and feelings. Few in the land would say what you, without blushing or apology for its insulting character and want of truthfulness, have said in the letter under consideration, about American citizens, in general, and about some of our most distinguished functionaries in State, in particular. You furnish, therefore, in my judgment, in your own case, a fair and full refutation of your assertions about the social intolerance of this land. But I must close. I have written to 'promote the welfare of my countrymen, and the advantage of my country,' by setting right what you had put wrong, and restoring order where you had produced confusion." AN OFFICER

Of the American and Foreign Christian Union.

NEW-YORK, February 26, 1853.

Reply by Simon Peter.

On the 11th of March, a little more than a week after the publication of the Reply by "an Officer of the American and Foreign Christian Union," the following, signed, "Simon Peter," was published in the New-York Herald. The writer is evidently well acquainted with the subject on which he writes, and his letter will be read with deep interest. It is humorous and instructive, and is worthy of particular attention. If it places the Archbishop and his cause in an unenviable position, the responsibility is on the Archbishop. He has placed it and himself there. But to the letter.

To the Rev. John Hughes, D. D.
Roman Catholic Archbishop of New-York.

Dear Sir,—Your Grace must not be surprised at receiving so much attention. It is one of the penalties of greatness to be exposed to such things. If you had not made yourself so conspicuous for aims already gratified, and higher ones yet to be accomplished—for the Archiepiscopate in possession, and the Cardinal's hat in expectation—I am not sure that what you say and do would arrest quite so much of the public notice as at present. In common with many others, I have read with some care your letter to the Freeman's Journal of the 19th instant, in relation to the "Madiai," the "Meeting in the Metropolitan Hall," "Religious liberty," etc. etc. and I must say that I was not a little disappointed. My dear Archbishop, many more "such deliverances" as the one in question, and that notable lecture on the "Decline of Protestantism," made just as you were about to set out on your late pilgrimage to Rome, will not augment your reputation either for logic or prudence.

The exordium of your Grace's letter was not happy. To attempt to ridicule the meeting in Metropolitan Hall, held for the purpose of expressing sympathy for poor and humble, but, nevertheless, very worthy people, who are suffering for doing what every man in these United States has the right to do—namely, to impart, by reading the Bible to his family and friends, and endeavoring to lead them to adopt his views of the Gospel, and act according to their convictions—very ill became the high and sacred office to which you claim to have been called by the Saviour of men; and because similar meetings had been held in England, it was poor logic to take it for granted that that meeting was held in imitation of them, and through admiration of the English aristocracy. It was not prudent for you to talk in this way, because your enemies may justly say that in this you betray your cherished antipathy to everything that is English. Your Irish origin will account for this. Had you been cognizant of the facts, you would have known that to imitate the English in this matter, or to have anything to do with any movement because it was English, was the last thing that would have occurred to any of the gentlemen with whom originated the meeting. On this point you are all wrong, I beg to assure your Eminence.

As to "ragged schools" for the poor children, which Ireland, not England, sends to our shores—which Romanism, not Protestantism, has made—our Protestant fellow-citizens, and among them the getters-up of the meeting at Metropolitan Hall, are not indifferent. They are doing much in many ways to care for them, but in a more Christian manner than the creating of ragged schools. But all this is of small moment; let us advance to more important topics.

The meeting was called to promote and express sympathy for the Madiai, and other sufferers (for the rights of conscience in the matter of religion) in the Grand Duchy of Tuscany, and for giving utterance to those principles, on the subject of religious liberty, which every true-hearted American both holds and feels, and which alone can either create or justify such sympathy. Nor can your Grace find any discrepancy between the objects set forth in the call for the meeting, signed by thirty distinguished Protestant gentlemen, and the statement of facts, resolutions, and series of propositions, presented to the public on the occasion. The meeting was called for the purposes just stated, and no other. As to what your Eminence says about the object being to abuse the Roman Catholic's of this country, and excite prejudice and animosity against them, etc. nothing more untrue was ever uttered by any man, and I can scarcely think that you believe the assertion. You have a marvellous tact for going off into whatever may divert men's minds from the true state of the case, whenever by so doing you can strengthen your cause. For was there anything said or read at the meeting which could be justly considered as calculated to excite prejudice against the Roman Catholics of this country. No one dreamed of holding them accountable for the acts of the Grand Duke of Tuscany in relation to the Madiai. It is true that the spirit and history of Rome, or rather of the Roman Catholic hierarchy—for it is the Roman Catholic Church, the people being nothing at all, and having nothing to do either in the determining of doctrines or the administration of discipline, as you well know—were spoken of freely by some of the speakers who endeavored to defend the Grand Duke of Tuscany, by saying truly that he is not so much to be blamed, or held accountable, for the infamous acts in question, as the priests around him, and especially Pio Nono, who could by a word terminate all this persecution. Some hard things were said about the hierarchy of Rome, it must be admitted; but they were just. It is also true that your eminence was most earnestly called on to join this movement in behalf of the poor sufferers, and exert your great influence to incline—by addressing him yourself, or praying his Holiness to do so—the heart of his Ducal majesty to leniency and grace. Surely there was nothing in all this like a premeditated plan, or any effort, to excite prejudice against our Roman Catholic fellow-citizens. The expressions of Dr. Bethune in favor of them were of the strongest character, and they were as real, as heartfelt, as they were strong.

No, sir; there was not a speaker on that occasion who dreamed of holding up the Roman Catholics of this country to reproach for the tyrannical acts of the Grand Duke of Tuscany. These gentlemen knew well that there are thousands among the Roman Catholics of this country, especially among those who were born in this land, as well as thousands in France, Germany, Italy, and other papal countries abroad, who condemn this outrageous injustice as earnestly as they themselves did or could. You, therefore, drew very largely on your imagination, dear Archbishop, when you spoke of the meeting as 'comprising a scurrilous denunciation of the Grand Duke of Tuscany, of the Jesuits, of the Pope, of the Catholic governments of Europe, of the Catholic citizens of the United States, and of the Catholic religion, and its members, of all times and places.'

The quoted words will indicate to your Grace the topics on which you have grossly (I will not say wilfully, for you and I are of Irish origin, and ought therefore to treat each other civilly) misrepresented the meeting, and those who spoke at it.

As to your complaint, that 'free discussion was shut off' at the meeting, you can hardly believe that it is well founded. Even your neophyte and *protegè*, the editor of the *Freeman's Journal*, could not have expected that his request to be allowed to speak, just as the meeting was coming to a close, and at the late hour of half-past ten o'clock, would or could be granted. The meeting was a meeting of the 'friends of religious liberty,' to which Roman Catholics and all others were invited, and so they and all the world understood the matter. Your Grace knows enough of such things to be convinced that such a meeting was not likely to be gotten up and carried on without some plan. And you know well, that if you and your Roman Catholic friends were to get up a public meeting of any nature, you would view as an intruder any man who would come in and claim the right of speaking without an invitation; and most certainly it is hard to conceive how your friend, the editor referred to, could expect to speak at the meeting in question, after all the abuse which he had heaped on the poor Madiai in the columns of his paper. But he and you, my good Archbishop, have it in your power to hold another public meeting, and set forth *your* views of religious liberty, and denounce persecution in Tuscany and everywhere else as much as you please, and Protestants will be there to hear you.

You are kind enough to say that you, too, would denounce the conduct of the Grand Duke of Tuscany if you could only believe that the Madiai have been imprisoned and made to suffer for 'reading their Bibles.' You cannot believe that this is the only cause of their being thus treated. Well, the case is a very simple one. These people read their Bibles, Diodati's version, a Protestant one, a translation from the original Hebrew and Greek, made by a scholar, a better one than Martini's, or any other Romish version in the Italian language—and in doing so they discovered the true Gospel, and abandoned the errors of Rome; they read the Bible to others, and imparted their convictions to their minds, and they, too, turned away from the Romish Church. This was the head and front of their offence. This was considered treason. Because they could not believe that the Virgin Mary is the mother of God, they were charged with blasphemy. They were tried and condemned on these grounds alone, and which two of their judges, (out of five,) and some of the ablest advocates in Florence, did not believe to be valid, even by the laws under which their condemnation was sought. Archbishop Hughes, do you believe—can you make this nation believe—that these people were justly condemned? You affect not to know anything about the circumstances of this case. Well, if you will look into the *Journal of Commerce* of February 14, 1852, you will find the accusation brought against these people at the time of their first imprisonment, and it will enlighten you somewhat. And, further, I have to say that we have sent for a copy of the proceedings at the trial, published in Italian, and when it arrives, we will appoint one competent man, and you shall be invited to appoint another, and these two shall appoint a third, and this committee shall determine whether these Madiai were condemned for a political offence, or for that which I have stated; the reading of their Bible, and endeavoring to impart their convictions on the subject of religion to others, not guilty of any political, or civil, or moral offence, against the laws of the land. You speak of their being condemned as if it were as a police affair. Yes, it was just such an affair of the police as that which put the Apostles in prison in Jerusalem, and which they expressly declared they would not, could not, obey. It was just such a police regulation as Prætors enforced at the bidding of their imperial masters at Rome, and which ten times deluged the empire with innocent Christian blood during the first three centuries.

You have given it as one reason why you cannot believe that the Madiai have been condemned for reading the Bible, that they have been allowed to read their Bible since their imprisonment; and you ask whether criminals—forgers, for instance—are allowed to continue their work of crime in prison after their condemnation? Mr. Moran, a Roman Catholic priest in Newark, New-Jersey, has asserted the same thing, and also, that they are allowed the visits of an ecclesiastic. But what are the facts? They are not allowed to have their own Protestant

Bible, (Diodati's,) nor their Protestant religious books and tracts, (although their confinement has been solitary most of the time,) but the Romish version of the Bible and Romish tracts are alone placed before them; and as to the ecclesiastic who is allowed to visit them regularly, he is a Capuchin monk!

Your Grace goes on to argue that your church cannot be—has never been—opposed to the reading of the Bible, because she has been from the first entrusted with the precious boon, or at least the New Testament, which is, in fact, her exclusive inheritance! This is very wonderful. Just as if the canon of sacred scripture was not settled, and every book of the sacred volume translated into almost all the important languages of Europe, Western Asia, and Northern Africa, long before the supremacy of the bishops of Rome was established, or the Roman Catholic Church heard of! Just as if the Greek Church, from the middle of the ninth century, and the five other Oriental Churches, had not the scriptures in their respective languages, and did not watch over them, and see to it that Rome did not corrupt them! There were other eyes than those of Rome, and other hands than hers, that cared for the precious treasure. I well know that after the art of printing was invented the Bible was published, not only in the original Hebrew and Greek, but also in the vernacular languages of Italy, Germany, Holland, France and England; but I have yet to learn that this was not rather the work of 'learned men,' than the result of the zeal of Rome, and her Popes, her Cardinals, her Archbishops and her Bishops. Indeed, some of the men who were engaged in this good work had a hard time of it. Even in the fifteenth century, the era of which I am speaking, Rome had departed too far from the truth contained in the written Word to have any relish for the sacred volume. The Reformation came, and it gave the Bible, in something like abundance, to the people, inasmuch as the Protestants regarded it as 'God's Book for the People.' But as to Rome—I mean the Roman Catholic Church, or hierarchy rather—she has not done much. Into what languages of the heathen, among whom her missionaries have labored these last two centuries, has the Bible been translated? In what has it been printed by those missionaries? Not many—I fear not one—I mean the whole Bible?

And where is there in all the world a Roman Catholic Bible society? If you know of one, pray tell me, my good Archbishop—tell me of one. You say that an Archbishop of Florence, Monsigneur Martini, translated the Bible into Italian in the year 1775. I know it. I have circulated many a copy of his New Testament, though I think it not equal to Diodati's, by a great deal. I have done so on the principle that an inferior translation is better than none. The British and Foreign Bible Society have printed both Diodati's and Martini's translations of the entire Bible, as well as the New Testament by itself.

Mr. Moran, a Roman Catholic priest, in Newark, New Jersey, already referred to, has recently affirmed that the Bible has not only been published in Italy, but that more than forty editions of Martini's translations have been issued since it was first published, and that it is to be seen in the bookstores in every village in Italy, from one end of the peninsula to the other. If this were so, one would think that far more than forty or fifty editions would have been needed. But it is not true. I know something of Italy; I have been there several times during the last sixteen years. Until the revolution of 1848 opened the way for the Bible Societies to print the Bible at Rome, Florence, Turin and Venice, the book was only to be seen in a few bookstores in the chief cities, and then in an edition of several octavo volumes, with copious notes, and costing several dollars. It is in vain to talk about the Bible being accessible to the people of Italy whilst published in that form. And though in 1848—'49 the Bible Societies did a good deal in Rome and Florence, yet as soon as the Pope and the Grand Duke had been restored from their flight by French and Austrian bayonets, everything of the sort was stopped. In Rome every house has been searched for the accursed book; and many copies have been confiscated and destroyed, both at Rome and at Florence. This is Rome's way of taking an interest in having the people to possess and read the Word of God. But you will say that it was a Protestant version of the New Testament that was confiscated in these cities. And what of that? It was a good version, and set forth the truth with great fidelity; but then it had not the authorized notes of the Church. Oh, yes; there is the rub. Rome is afraid to give the Bible, just as God gave it, to the people. She must put notes to it to interpret certain passages as she thinks proper. Well, this Italian New Testament, with abundant notes, has been published, in two large editions, in a convenient form, and at a comparatively reasonable price, at Turin, within the last two years, but by a bookseller—his Grace, the Archbishop of that city, having nothing to do in the matter. Indeed, his Grace has not been at home these two or three years, the government of Sardinia having given him permission to travel into foreign parts, because of his having improperly meddled with political affairs and endeavored to subvert the constitution!

Your Grace cites, in proof of the interest which your Church takes in the people's possessing and reading the Bible, the fact that some twenty or twenty-five editions have been published (of the Roman Catholic version) in various sizes, and under proper episcopal supervision, in these United States.

This is a most extraordinary and fatal statement. Why, if we suppose that each edition was of 10,000 copies, (which is probably very far beyond the mark,) then no more than 250,000 copies in all of the Roman Catholic version, (not half as many as our American Bible Society issues in one year,) have been published in this country, for the now two or three millions of Romanists. Archbishop, Archbishop! this is too bad! And yet, what better could be expected? Notwithstanding all you have said in your recent "Letter," you know that your Church is not in favor of giving the Bible to the people, excepting under conditions which render the permission of very little value. Let me ask you whether you have not, within a few months, in a sermon at Yonkers, New-York, said to the people that they ought not to read the Bible—that they could not understand it—that the Church alone has the ability and the right to explain the Bible—that it is enough for the people to learn the catechism, and believe what the Church says to them by the mouth of the priest? Did you not say this, or what was equivalent to it? If you did not, some gentlemen of my acquaintance greatly misunderstood you.

As to your remarks about 'liberty of conscience,' I have not much to say. You might well have spared the little homily, for everybody knows that liberty of conscience does not mean liberty to hold and enjoy one's conscientious opinions on the subject of religion to one's self, but the right to make them known to others. The nature of truth is to seek to be known—in other words, to make proselytes. 'A Catholic Layman,' in the New-York *Times* of the 24th ult. has well stated that fact. He has also well distinguished between the liberty which is created by the constitution and laws, and that which prevails in the feelings and habits of communities. The religious liberty granted to all by our constitution and laws is complete; and yet occasionally popular excitement may be gotten up, which, for a time, set aside the laws, and overthrow the liberty guaranteed by the constitution and the laws. You endeavor to throw dust in the eyes of your readers by disregarding these important distinctions; and would make them almost believe that we have not religious liberty in this land, because damage has been done, in popular tumults, to a Roman Catholic convent near Boston, and a church or two in Philadelphia. Because men cannot say and publish in South Carolina and Louisiana what they please on the subject of slavery, you insinuate that there is not entire religious liberty in this country. If you will allow me to say it, I think that it is altogether unworthy of you. You know that there is religious liberty in this land; that in no State in this Union is a man forbidden to buy a Bible, if he has the means; he may read it if he can; and if he is so unfortunate as to be unable to read, whether owing to any unwise laws in any State, or any other cause, he may hear it read, he may hear the Gospel preached, believe, and decide for himself what church he will join. Would that there was as much religious liberty as this in all Roman Catholic countries? As to the religious liberty which Roman Catholics enjoy in this country, you seem to think that they are in no way indebted to Protestants for it—that they fought for it during the Revolution, and gained it by their good, trusty swords. This is also very wonderful. Just as if the Revolution in which the Roman Catholics—though they were too few to have much influence in that great movement—certainly bore their parts, (and some of them, such as Charles Carroll and a few others, a very honorable one,) gave religious liberty to this country. You must certainly know, dear Archbishop, that all the colonies brought hither the germ of religious liberty, whether they came from England, Scotland, France or Germany, though in some it was more developed than in others. But all went on advancing in regard to this great subject until the Revolution, when all the thirteen colonies, Protestant, (even Maryland was so,) by an overwhelming majority, enjoyed a great amount of religious liberty, and some of them a full measure. It was this fact which insured the incorporation of the principle of religious liberty into the constitution. Nothing is more certain than that all the religious liberty there is in the world is owing to Protestantism. As to the statement which your Grace has sometimes made, that we owe our religious liberty to the little colony which Lord Baltimore planted in Maryland, it is hardly worthy of consideration. From the nature of the case, that colony could not fail to have religious liberty from the first; for a Protestant government in England never would have allowed a Roman Catholic colony to be planted here upon the principle of intolerance. But if, as you say, Rome is favorable to religious liberty, why does she not grant it in her own domain? Why does she not?

I cannot doubt the attachment of our Roman Catholic fellow-citizens to our noble political institutions. And yet I could not read what you say about their "well-poised self-possession," that kept them from being carried away by the influence of a "foreign demagogue" (Kossuth) who recently visited us, without something more than a smile. Oh, Archbishop! if Kossuth had been a Roman Catholic, or contending against a Protestant country, you would, perhaps, have thought differently of him. But he was a Protestant, who had tried to overthrow the despotism of the House of Hapsburg, (which has been a good servant and friend of the Papacy,) and in doing so he had the generous aid of millions of Roman Catholics of his country, far more than half of the soldiers and officers who fought in that war being such. But he fought against Austria! That was enough. But let us look at the other side. Where was the "well-poised self-possession" of the Irish Roman Catholics in this country—where was your own, dearest Archbishop—in the summer of 1848, when the last rebellion broke out in Ireland? Surely your memory cannot be very good. Have you not forgotten those $500 which you gave to kindle the flame of civil war in your native land? But then it was to overthrow the dominion of hated Protestant Albion in the Emerald Isle. That changed the whole affair. But let us talk no more about the matter, for I greatly fear that it is not agreeable to you.

Nor am I sure that the next topic will be any more so. You have berated General Cass, and others, for endeavoring to secure the protection of our American citizens, in their religious rights, in foreign lands. Now, this measure is so just and equal, that I wonder that a man of your penetration does not see that people will say to you: "Yes, you know that American Roman Catholics, as well as American Protestants, are protected in their rights in Protestant countries almost as much as they can desire, and that in most Roman Catholic countries American Protestants have not the right to have their own religious worship, and to bury their dead with such ceremonies as they prefer, and therefore you are quite contented with the present state of things—from the feeling that Protestantism has something to lose, and Romanism nothing, through its influence." This is precisely what every intelligent Protestant will think and say about your conduct in this matter. And what do you think of it yourself, my dear Archbishop? Does it not appear rather too mean and contemptible? I feel concerned for you.

Still further: what shall we think of your opposing the interference of Mr. Fillmore in behalf of the Madiai, especially when you, and hundreds of others, asked this same President Fillmore to do precisely what he has now done in favor of Smith O'Brien and other Irish rebels—or "patriots," if you prefer the word—that is, write a letter of intercession in their behalf to the Queen of England? What a "degradation" this, for our noble President and our immortal Webster, to be seen standing in humble attendance in the ante-chamber of Albion's proud monarch; and all this for a few Irishmen, for whom you would have said, if they had been Hungarians, that "hanging was too good for them." "Oh, consistency, thou art a jewel!"—but not, in this case, an *Irish* one.

But you seem to make it a matter of reproach to our great meeting at Metropolitan Hall, that none of the great Protestant pastors of the city of New-York took part in the speaking on the occasion. The orators were all from such "suburban villages" as Brooklyn, Newark, and Elizabethtown. If the Hall could have been obtained for Monday night, instead of Friday, it is quite probable that you would have heard, had you been there, (it is reported that you were,) some gentlemen from the city who were that night occupied with the irregular weekly lectures. As it was, the meeting went off pretty well. The "suburbans" acquitted themselves decently, all of them. They are no mean men; nor are they all unknown to your Grace. Dr. Bethune made the audience feel that he was well able to grapple with the subject. Drs. Kennedy, Hague, and Cox, certainly did not disgrace themselves. And as to "Kirwan," I think your Grace has some remembrance of him, unless your "hegira to Halifax" made you as oblivious of the past as is the "Bourbon among us" of the occurrences of his early days.

But, with your permission I will stop here, at least until your Eminence favors the public with another "letter" on some subject or other.

I am, your Grace's most humble and obedient servant, SIMON PETER.

Why have the Madiai been treated so cruelly?

We cannot allow this volume to be completed without giving the testimony of our countryman, the Rev. G. H. Hastings, in behalf of these excellent people. Mr. Hastings was the American Chaplain at Rome for three years. In a series of letters published in the *New York Commercial Advertiser* in the month of April, 1853, he has given many interesting particulars respecting both Francesco and Rosa Madiai. The former he saw often at his house, as well as in the American Chapel, at Rome, during the winter of 1850–51. On one occasion Sig. Madiai officiated as a deacon for Mr. Hastings, in the administration of the Lord's Supper. Mr. H. describes him as being a very pleasant, dignified, gentlemanly person, of much good sense, and remarkably acquainted with the Scriptures. He was a zealous and faithful Christian, very decidedly evangelical in his views, and possessing great tact and skill in controversial discussions. He took little or no interest in politics, his mind being engrossed with the spiritual, rather than the political, regeneration of Italy. He was in Rome in the capacity of a courier to some English ladies of great respectability—a post which is of much responsibility and requiring great attention, kindness of manner, and fidelity. Mr. Hastings saw Madame Madiai at Florence in June following, and describes her as a woman much superior to most women of her position in society. Tall, slender, dignified, energetic—though in delicate health—she was altogether a remarkable person. She was prudent as well as zealous. Her long residence in England had given her correct ideas of the nature and importance of constitutional government; but politics occupied not her attention. She was more concerned for the enlightenment of her people in the knowledge of God's Word. Mr. H. thinks, however, that if only half of the men in Tuscany had been born of such women as Rosa Madiai, there would soon be no Austrians in that duchy—and we think so too.

We subjoin the reasons which Mr. Hastings has given for the harsh and severe manner in which the Madiai have been treated by the Tuscan government. We have no doubt that he has stated the case justly.

"In respect to distributing Bibles, the Madiai were certainly active, but not as agents of any society whatever; nor had they ever any large number of Bibles and Testaments deposited with them. It was not their practice to thrust copies upon those who might not desire them; but to procure them from time to time for such as they found disposed to search them honestly.

"The tracts, which they circulated with the same prudence, were all published at Florence with the approval of the censorship in 1849, and contained nothing with which a truly pious Romanist could feel offended; they having been prepared with great care to present the pure Gospel only, without controversy.

"In respect to proselytism, it must be admitted that both conversed freely with such as came naturally under their influence, and were willing to listen to them. In this matter they kept quietly within the circle of common social intercourse, never putting themselves forward as zealots. They employed none of those arts which characterize the proselyter in the offensive sense of the word, as one must naturally observe from reading the specifications under this head in their sentence. Four cases are cited in proof of their 'scandalous conduct,' as the judge termed it; three of them of domestics in their family, and the other a young man of sixteen, to whom Mr. M. gave French lessons; all of which persons at the time expressed themselves grateful for the instruction and advice offered them, though not all were directly influenced by it.

"In their defence, the Madiai said that they never attempted anything of this kind except where they found spiritual stupidity and ignorance; and that in striving to win souls to the knowledge of Christ, they must necessarily do it after the manner in which they had learned him.

"Finally, as the very worst which the government could make out against them, they were found guilty of having 'insinuated the preference which the religion called Evangelical deserved over the Catholic, and counselling that one should not give heed to the teachings of the priests; reprobating the worship of the Virgin, and of the saints, as idolatry, and ridi culing particularly the pious custom of keeping a light burning before the sacred image of the former.'

"That they used this and similar language hundreds of times in the course of the three years, from 1848 to 1851, when there was a growing Protestant feeling around them, is true enough. But that they ever occasioned any disturbance by it, either in the street, or at any public resort, or in private dwellings, is not pretended by their accusers; and certain it is that they never indulged in that virulent language toward the priesthood common to the people of Italy.

"If then the Madiai were such persons as I have described them to be, humble, unobtrusive, and scrupulous to avoid, if possible, violating the known laws of the land, why were they treated with such extraordinary severity? I answer, they were the victims of State policy. Both the Court of Tuscany and the Court of Rome considered it necessary, for the extirpation of the spreading heresy, to make such an example of some respectable individuals as should strike terror among the people. Count Guicciardini was too powerful for them, and had, moreover, been too prudent to give them a sufficiently plausible excuse for anything more than a sentence of exile for six months.

"The other individuals arrested had been too insignificant for their purpose. Examinations and the testimony of spies, pointed to the house of the Madiai as the favorite resort of the Evangelical dissenters. The family, moreover, had a certain reputation with the English, who would feel the blow which should descend upon it. From the moment the government saw this, no degree of prudence on their part could have saved them. The occasion of the arrest of Mr. Madiai was, as we have seen, the merest pretence on the part of the police; but that was no matter; his fate was already determined upon. The Duke, the Duchess, and various members of the Court were known to have said repeatedly, that they would make such an example of this family as should effectually terrify others from embracing the Evangelical faith. The decree of 1787, under which they were condemned for 'impiety,' did not apply to their case; but that also was no matter; the Inquisition claimed them, and the laws of their country could not protect them. Agreeably to the concordat signed at Rome on the 25th of April, 1851, the sentence of the Madiai was 'deferred to the ecclesiastical authorities,' and was actually approved at Rome before being pronounced at Florence. This, Count Baldasseroni, then Minister of State, will not deny.

"Well have the Grand Duke and the Grand Duchess fulfilled their vow. They have made an example of the Madiai. But an example of what? Why, of what poor Italy had well nigh forgotten; the simplicity of the primitive Christian faith, and the true martyr spirit.

"But what have these princes, at the same time,

made of themselves? Let the indignant remonstrances made to them by Cabinets, Legislative Assemblies, and the people of half of Christendom, answer. They have vowed to extirpate from their dominions this 'confession called Evangelical, or the pure Gospel,' though their names go down to posterity clothed with the odium of a Nero. The odium they are gathering fast; but the confession, being indeed that of the Pure Gospel, has only become the better appreciated by their subjects for their persecution of it."

We cannot forbear to give the following remarks which Mr. Hastings makes in the concluding number of the letters referred to. They are just, and their importance will be acknowledged by all reasonable men.

"A word in conclusion respecting the certain consequences of the imprisonment of the Madiai, which are beginning to show themselves in this country. There was reason to fear that so long as their humble and sincere confessors of the evangelical faith remained in bonds for conscience sake, there would be continual outbreaks of popular will toward Romanism, to the just grievance of our Roman Catholic fellow-citizens. Such a result every enlightened patriot, Protestant or Catholic, would have endeavored to avert. As Protestants we are bound to defend the religious freedom here enjoyed by the Romanists; as their fellow-citizens we are bound to respect their equal title to every civil privilege known to us. Moreover, we are so extensively linked together in social ties of relationship and love, that either party must necessarily feel outraged at any indignity cast upon the other. But at this juncture, when popular passion is becoming excited at the barbarity of Roman Catholic Governments abroad, with whom rests the greatest power to tranquillize the public mind? Let the Roman Catholic clergy and editors candidly admit the violence done to all just liberty of conscience in the treatment of the Madiai; let them show that they have no sympathy with the Tuscan Government in this persecution of dissenters; and join us in our endeavors or make some honest effort of their own, to cause religious persecution everywhere to cease; and they will accomplish quickly, and with ease, a change in the popular feeling which millions of Protestants in their best endeavors, and the civil authorities with all their forces, can never effect. But let them persist in their attempts to make false issue in this case by their wretched sophisms in commendation of the Grand Duke, and in derogation of the Madiai; let them continue to denounce the active sympathy of the Protestant world in behalf of these sufferers for Christ's sake as 'all a farce,' and let them still contemn 'as mere drivelling' the efforts of our national Cabinet, of our Senators and State Legislatures, to procure by treaty the right of public worship for American citizens in Roman Catholic countries—then will they make themselves the most guilty agents of all, in kindling the flame of popular wrath toward Romanism. Nor, in such case, can the people avoid the conviction that the claims of Romanism here, as well as on the continent, and the secret agency of the priesthood too, are utterly at war with the free institutions of the country?

"The principles upon which the Roman Catholic sovereigns of Europe, instigated by the Court of Rome, are now acting toward the poor people, and toward Protestants in particular, are in the highest degree oppressive, unjust and cruel; as opposite to the precepts of the Saviour as depraved human nature can make them. The great mass of our Roman Catholic fellow-citizens secretly believe this; but they are restrained from the public expression of their convictions. May they yet have bishops and editors who will know how to disengage the religion of Jesus from all fellowship with such principles, and who may be able to guide the Roman Catholic mind of the country into just views and the perfect practice of religious toleration. Then shall we walk peaceably together; and the excesses of sectarian strife, which we have too much reason to dread, will be averted."

THEIR LIBERATION.

CONCLUSION.

The Deputation from England, France, Holland, Germany, and Switzerland, visited Tuscany in October 1852, about the same time the King of Prussia, it is understood, wrote a letter to the Grand Duke, and sent one of his favorite Councellors of State to intercede in behalf of these suffering ones. It is believed that the Queen of England caused her earnest desires for their liberation, to be made known to his "Imperial and Ducal Highness." But all seems to be in vain, so far as their release was concerned. It is true that these efforts in their behalf, together with the great publicity which was given through the Journals, to the reports made by the Deputation, as well as by other persons who gained access to their prisons, probably had no little influence in securing for the prisoners the humane treatment which, according to Mr. Colombe, the Swiss Chaplain at Florence, they undoubtedly received during the latter and greater portion of their confinement after their condemnation. So much was gained; but still there was no manifestation of a disposition on the part of the Government to release them.

This was the state of things when the great meeting in Metropolitan Hall, New-York, on the 7th

January, 1853; followed by those in Newark, New Jersey! and Baltimore, not long afterwards. By the Steam Ship of January 6th, the letter of the Hon. Edward Everett, was forwarded to the Grand Duke of Tuscany. This letter was *unofficial*, and sent to the American Consul at Florence, with directions to cause it to reach the Grand Duke. About two weeks later Lord John Russel, the British Minister for Foreign Affairs, addressed an earnest and very stringent letter to Mr. Bulwer, the English Ambassador at Florence, and directing him to use all the influence he could in behalf of the prisoners.

Through God's blessing, these efforts were not in vain. The Grand Duke at length resolved to liberate them, and send them out of the country. Without a word said to the British Ambassador, or the least notice given to the public, the prisoners were sent down to Leghorn by different trains on the rail-road. Madame Madiai, from Lucca on Tuesday, March 22nd, and her husband from Florence the day following. Upon her arrival at Leghorn, Madame Madiai was taken to the French Consulate, whence she was ordered to go at once on board a French Mail Steamer, which was to leave the next day for Marsailles. This she refused positively to do; saying that she was a *Tuscan*, and not a *French* subject, and that the French Consul had no right to send her out of the country. This ground was also taken, it is probable, from an apprehension that *she* was to be liberated, and her husband left in prison. Upon the Consul's solemn assurance that her husband would join her the day following on board the Steamer, she consented to embark. From the steamer she contrived to send a parcel and a *note* to the British Consul, informing him of what was going on, and requesting him to come and see her,—which he immediately did, accompanied by the English Chaplain. The latter wrote at once to the London "Times," and the former telegraphed Mr. Erskine, the British Charge' d'Affaires at Florence, who lost no time in communicating the fact to Lord John Russell, which fact he stated in the House of Commons on the Friday following.

On Wednesday, March 23d, Francesco Madiai was sent down to Leghorn, accompanied by M. de Gabriac, the French Ambassador at Florence, and was immediately placed on board the Steamer referred to. There he met his wife, *just nineteen months, that day, after their arrest and first imprisonment!* The British Consul took pains to supply them both with suitable clothing, of which they ha.. great need, for the weather was very inclement, and they had only the light dresses in which they were sent to their last prisons in July. The French Ambassador and Consul went with them to Marseilles, and committed them to the care of the Police of that city—a fact which has led some to believe that they owe their liberation to the interposition of the

French Government.—Indeed, they were so informed by these gentlemen on the Steamer, although it would be difficult to reconcile all this with the previous conduct and language of M. de Gabriac. It is more likely that they were requested to accompany the liberated ones for the purpose of securing their admission into France, and a proper disposition of them there.

Both Francesco and Rosa Madiai were exceedingly debilitated by their long imprisonment; and their first desire was to find repose at Marseilles. They were received with kindness by the Prefect of the Department, (Bouches du Rhone,) who kindly permitted them to attend Protestant worship,(which the Police were disposed to prevent, because their presence attracted a crowd,) and to enjoy themselves as best they could. At the time of this writing it is not known to us where they will take up their abode. It is probable that after spending some time in the south of France, they will go to Switzerland. They have been invited to England and to Prussia. They will find a welcome in any Protestant country—in none a more heart-felt one than in our own, if they should wish to come to us.

Here we bring our STORY OF THE MADIAI to an end. What an illustration of the infernal spirit of Rome? What a proof that even in this Nineteenth Century she is just what she was when in successive ages she persecuted the Albigences, the Waldenses, the Hussites, and the Protestants of France, Flanders, Italy, Poland, and Hungary! Well may the dear liberated ones exclaim: *The snare is broken, and we are escaped!* There is reason to believe that whatever may be done hereafter in Tuscany to extirpate *heresy* will be done in a secret manner, and in accordance with the recent edicts of the Government, which give the Police unbounded power to arrest and imprison without a trial! Already they are making that power to be felt. Well may we exclaim: *How long, O Lord, how long?*

THE END.

www.ingramcontent.com/pod-product-compliance
Lightning Source LLC
LaVergne TN
LVHW020246110826
845151LV00003B/1026
* 9 7 8 1 4 2 5 5 2 9 6 0 4 *